"One cannot understand our world today without appreciating the role of religion in global affairs. Drawing upon a rich background in teaching religious studies and interreligious engagement, Terry Muck offers wise, perceptive, and helpful guidance for studying religious traditions. This is a terrific treatment of a crucial subject."

—**Harold Netland**, Trinity Evangelical Divinity School

"Why study religion? Senior scholar and statesman Terry Muck answers this question, drawing on his years of teaching, research, and dialogue with diverse religious practitioners. Ideal for classroom use, this well-rounded, practical, and clearly written text is timely in its import as those living in North America must learn to navigate astutely the waters of our vital and volatile religiously plural culture. Highly recommended."

—**Paul Louis Metzger**, Multnomah University; author of *Connecting Christ: How to Discuss Jesus in a World of Diverse Paths*

WHY
STUDY
RELIGION?

UNDERSTANDING HUMANITY'S
PURSUIT OF THE DIVINE

TERRY C. MUCK

B
Baker Academic
a division of Baker Publishing Group
Grand Rapids, Michigan

Published by Baker Academic
a division of Baker Publishing Group
P.O. Box 6287, Grand Rapids, MI 49516-6287
www.bakeracademic.com

Printed in the United States of America

Library of Congress Cataloging-in-Publication Data
Names: Muck, Terry C., 1947– author.
Title: Why study religion? : understanding humanity's pursuit of the divine / Terry C. Muck.
Description: Grand Rapids : Baker Academic, 2016. | Includes bibliographical references and index.
Identifiers: LCCN 2016004352 | ISBN 9780801049958 (pbk.)
Subjects: LCSH: Religion—Study and teaching. | Religion—Methodology.
Classification: LCC BL41 .M84 2016 | DDC 200.71—dc23
LC record available at http://lccn.loc.gov/2016004352

16   17   18   19   20   21   22   7   6   5   4   3   2   1

To Frances,
whose community I share,
whose love I enjoy,
who fills my life with grace.

Contents

Study Aids

Preface

Why study religion? Because religion is important. While the type and the quality of the religion being practiced certainly influence the rise and fall of explicitly spiritual concerns, both politics and economics are also affected by religious currents. No matter what part of the world we are talking about, no matter what specific religion is under discussion, rest assured that religion is an indispensable part of what is going on. Why is the study of religion important? Because religion helps us to understand the world better. Consequently, this book argues for the importance of studying religion.

Who is this book written for? For students and scholars of religion, especially those living in Western cultures. For those just starting out in their quest to understand religion. For students taking their first course in religion—such as an Introduction to World Religion course, which is regularly offered in colleges, universities, and theological schools. The pages that follow show new students and nascent scholars why it is important to study religion and how to go about this important task.

This book might also serve as a refresher for advanced students who have already taken a few courses in religious studies or for those who have decided to choose religious studies as a vocation. Senior scholars already teaching religious studies to others may even find the book useful. All three of these groups—advanced students, students in doctoral programs in religion, and senior scholars—obviously know more than just a little about the religions of the world and the people who adhere to them. For these readers, this book is a way to step back and see what they know and what they have yet to learn.

The words *student* and *scholar* are connected to each other. In certain situations, they can be used as terms of progression; at some point, a student who studies and learns becomes a scholar who researches and teaches. In this book, I prefer to see *student* and *scholar* as synonyms rather than terms of position or rank. Better yet, they can be modifiers of each other: student-scholars and scholar-students. Scholars never stop studying and learning. Students, even very new ones, do research. What's more, students teach; those of us who have taught religious studies are forever learning from those in our classes. A student can be a scholar, and a scholar is forever a student.

Why did I write this book? I love religious studies. Last year I retired after teaching religious studies for a quarter of a century. My little corner of the religious studies vineyard was teaching theological students to understand religions other than Christianity. I specialized in Buddhism, especially Theravada Buddhism and Buddhist-Christian interactions. I taught courses at Austin Presbyterian Theological Seminary, Asbury Theological Seminary, and Louisville Presbyterian Theological Seminary—many courses, hundreds of students—and I experienced a great deal of enjoyment and satisfaction doing so. I hope that a sense of that enjoyment and satisfaction comes through on the pages that follow.

To whom am I grateful? To my colleagues at Austin Seminary, Asbury Seminary, and Louisville Seminary. To my students at those schools. To interlocutors and friends in the Society for Buddhist Christian Studies. To religious studies scholars long past and present, who have taught me through both word and deed. And to Frances. I am blessed.

Terry Muck
Wood Hill, August 2015

Introduction

If this book is to adequately answer the question of its title, *Why Study Religion?*, it is essential to begin with a simple and clear statement of what religion is. Unfortunately, there is nothing simple or clear about defining religion.[1] The definition of religion and/or a religion is a contentious topic. For the purposes of this book, however, *religion* is defined as a set of human practices that provides for its adherents answers to four questions:

> What is the ideal state of life?
> What has gone wrong?
> What can put things right?
> How should we then live?

This kind of definition (which I will refer to as the Four-Question Definition) is useful when one is trying to describe the boundaries and purposes of human behavior operating in the religious mode. What do I mean by "religious mode"? When humans ask and answer ultimate questions having to do with both the real and perceived shortcomings of life and the eradication of those shortcomings, they

1. See Paul Mandeville and Paul James, *Globalizing Religions* (London: Sage, 2010).

1

are being religious. They are in religious mode. The story related to these questions and answers—the beliefs that story engenders and the everyday virtues the story encourages—is a person's religion.

This kind of definition helps us to identify what both groups and individuals consider their religion to be.[2] It is designed to include the extraordinary variety of explicit human religious traditions (e.g., Hinduism, Buddhism, Islam, Confucianism, etc.) as well as implicit religious intuitions (i.e., ways of being and living that may not be recognized as religious systems, per se, but function as such in people's lives).[3]

One semester, after giving a lecture that included the Four-Question Definition for religion and its rationale, a member of the class came up to me and said, "According to your definition of religion, at this point in my life, Alcoholics Anonymous is functioning as my religion." Together, we considered his statement. His life was consumed with his out-of-control drinking, even though he knew that sobriety was the ideal state. Unfortunately, his addiction to alcohol prevented him from achieving the ideal. Attending AA meetings and getting support from other similarly afflicted group members was a way to help him work toward that goal. A twelve-step program of spiritual and character development set out in some detail how he needed to live his life in order to be sober. For him, AA was his implicit religion.

To be sure, AA is not recognized as a religious tradition in the same way that Judaism, Christianity, Islam, Hinduism, Buddhism, Confucianism, Taoism, and others are. The differences are obvious. Alcoholics Anonymous is a relatively new movement, founded in 1935 by Bill Wilson and Bob Smith.[4] While it does not claim to be

2. These are sometimes called family definitions, a name derived from the concept of "family resemblances," which was developed by Ludwig Wittgenstein in his *Philosophical Investigations* (London: Wiley-Blackwell, 1953). "Family resemblance" describes overlapping similarities that connect a group of things or ideas, as opposed to a single essential, common feature. Wittgenstein's example is games rather than religions, but the application to religion is spot on.

3. Implicit religions are human commitments that at first glance appear to be secular, but closer examination reveals that they may contain a religion of their own. See E. I. Baily, *Implicit Religion in Contemporary Society* (Leuven, Belgium: Peeters, 1997).

4. In 1939 Wilson and some colleagues wrote a book that became the "bible" of the AA movement: *Alcoholics Anonymous*, 4th ed. (New York: Alcoholics Anonymous World Service, 2001). Sometimes referred to as "the Big Book," it outlines twelve steps

a religion, it can be an effective way to increase human flourishing among a population of people who have often given up hope of finding any kind of enduring meaning. The advantage of a definition of religion that can include both explicit and implicit religion is its focus on what religions really do. At their best, religions provide meaning in the swelter of meaninglessness in which most of us live; religions provide hope to the hopeless. This way of defining religion is strong because it gives as wide a scope as possible to what might be considered religious among the global human population.

Other Types of Definitions of Religion: Research Definitions

The Four-Question Definition of religion is, however, not the best way to define religion if the goal of the definition is to provide scope and boundaries of a different sort. If the goal of a definition of religion is *limitation* (for the purposes of research) rather than *inclusiveness*, then a different set of definitions is available. That's right, a *set* of definitions, plural. The primary difficulty in defining religion is its vast reach across all human life.[5] The only way to attempt to define religion in its entirety and diversity is to use the Four-Question Definition, also called the family definition (see note 2 in this chapter). In order to do scholarly research and observation of religion, however, one needs to limit the scope of religious behavior, not expand it. Different scholars choose to hive off manageable chunks of human religious behavior, typically using the methodologies of ancillary scholarly fields of inquiry.[6] Psychologists of religion limit their research

alcoholics can take to help them toward sobriety, the first of which is to admit they are addicted and powerless. The twelve steps suggest seeking guidance and strength from God or some other higher power through prayer and meditation.

5. Diana Eck, professor of world religions at Harvard University, is famous for having said that her introductory course in world religions is impossible to teach because, properly done, it would cover all human activity and history from the beginning of time. Although the quote may be apocryphal and only playfully ascribed to Eck, I agree with its basic sentiment, having taught introduction to world religions courses for over twenty-five years.

6. Although there is no precise list of the disciplines and the methodologies that have been used by religious studies scholars, the sixteen-volume *Encyclopedia of*

energies to individual human behavior, while sociologists of religion focus on group behaviors, anthropologists of religion look to cultural patterns, and philosophers of religion concentrate on belief systems. When historians of religions, psychologists of religion, sociologists of religion, and others do their research, they use narrower definitions of religion in order to limit their subject matter and field of research. Consider the following examples of these types of definitions.

From an anthropologist of religion, Clifford Geertz:

> Religion is (1) a system of symbols which acts to (2) establish powerful, pervasive, and long-lasting moods and motivations in men by (3) formulating conceptions of a general order of existence and (4) clothing these conceptions with such an aura of factuality that (5) the moods and motivations seem uniquely realistic.[7]

From a sociologist of religion, Émile Durkheim:

> A religion is a unified system of beliefs and practices relative to sacred things, that is to say, things set apart and forbidden—beliefs and practices which unite into one single moral community called a Church, all those who adhere to them.[8]

From a psychologist of religion, William James:

> Religion is the feelings, acts, and experiences of individual men in their solitude, so far as they apprehend themselves to stand in relation to whatever they may consider the divine.[9]

Religion, ed. Mircea Eliade (New York: Macmillan, 1987) includes: anthropology, archaeology, ecology, ethnoastronomy, evolutionism, functionalism, history, *kulturkreislehre*, mythology, phenomenology, philosophy, psychology, *religionsgeschichtliche schule*, sociology, ritual studies, sociology, structuralism, comparative theology, and women's studies.

7. Clifford Geertz, "Religion as a Cultural System," in *The Interpretation of Cultures* (New York: Fontana, 1974), 90.

8. Émile Durkheim, *The Elementary Forms of the Religious Life* (London: George Allen and Unwin, 1915), 44.

9. William James, *The Varieties of Religious Experience* (Mineola, NY: Dover, 2002), 31.

From a philosopher of religion, Immanuel Kant:

> Religion is the recognition of all our duties as divine commands.[10]

In this book, I will use the family definition (the Four-Question Definition) in most instances but will occasionally make reference to the more specific, research-oriented definitions. In the study of religion, one is not looking for the single, right definition of religion but for the definition that fits what one is attempting to do as a scholar of religion. The important thing is to be clear about how one defines religion at any specific time, in any specific project. In a sense, religion scholars are pluralists when it comes to defining religion because there can be many right answers. One of these answers includes so-called theological definitions of religion, which brings us into another arena of thought.

The Subject Matter of Religious Studies

In order to explore this arena, let's go back to the writings of Max Müller, a nineteenth-century Oxford University linguist whom many consider the father of the modern academic discipline of religious studies (what Müller calls the "science of religion"). In explaining precisely what he considers the subject matter of the "science of religion" to be, Müller distinguishes three types of religion.

Pathological religion refers not only to the evil uses to which cultures and cultural leaders put the religious traditions of the world but also to the evil effect such religious systems can sometimes have on human flourishing and on individual human personalities. As Müller puts it (anticipating a trend of the New Atheists, which is discussed below), "There are philosophers, no doubt, to whom both Christianity and all other religions are exploded errors, things belonging to the past, and to be replaced by more positive knowledge. To them the study of the religions of the world could only have a pathological interest."[11]

---

10. Immanuel Kant, *Religion and Rational Theology* (London: Cambridge University Press, 2001), 177.
11. Max Müller, *Chips from a German Workshop*, vol. 1 (1869; repr., Chico, CA: Scholars Press, 1985), xxxi.

Natural religion refers to the narrative of religious faith told by and made manifest in all the cultures of the world and in the individuals who represent those cultures at all times of human history and across the entire geographical spread of human history. Natural religion is what can be read about, observed in human behavior, and philosophically analyzed.

Revealed religion refers to the extra-natural originations and manifestations of religion that have their beginnings in a transcendent realm yet produce tangible effects in the natural world and in the lives of human beings and their cultures. As Müller writes: "There are other philosophers, again, who would fain narrow the limits of the Divine government of the world to the history of the Jewish and of the Christian nations, who would grudge the very name of religion to the ancient creeds of the world, and to whom the name of natural religion has almost become a term of reproach."[12]

Müller taught that his developing "science of religion" was designed primarily to study what he calls natural religion.[13] Although the science of religion does not exclude the acknowledgment that religion has been and still is sometimes used for pathological purposes and that the origin of religion may indeed be in some transcendent realm, Müller says that neither the pathological nor the revealed expressions of religion are as amenable to scientific study as the natural, everyday expressions of religion. I agree with Müller that (what he calls) natural religion is the focus of the religious studies scholar, with pathological and revealed religion as only secondary research topics. Why natural religion? Why not pathological religion or revealed religion? To answer these questions, let's discuss each of the three forms in more detail, using Müller's understandings and then expanding those understandings to our current day and age.

12. Ibid.

13. That Müller has two names for the field of study he is proposing—the "science of religion" and "natural religion"—points to the many names this field has been called in its brief history. In addition to Müller's designations, it has been called comparative religion, history of religion, *religionwissenschaft*, and *sciences des religions*, among others. Although the most common designation today is religious studies, it is not uncommon to find departments in universities with other nomenclatures. For example, I studied at Northwestern University where our department was called the History and Literature of Religions.

Regarding *pathological religion*, it might be more accurate to say that Müller objects to reducing all religion to pathology. Using either a psychological or sociological understanding of pathology and claiming that one of the two explains all of religion as a starting point is, of course, possible to do. Two of the most fertile thinkers of the nineteenth and twentieth centuries, Sigmund Freud and Karl Marx, did just that. Psychologist Freud began with the assumption that all religion is an illusion, a projection and extension of childhood love of parents that is carried over into adulthood.[14] Sociologist Marx assumed that all religion is an opiate, which is administered to the proletariat by the bourgeoisie to keep the former in the iron grip of the latter.[15]

Müller argues that studying religion as a pathology not only prejudges the issue but also does not hold true in terms of what one discovers by looking objectively at the religions of the world and the overall effects they have on the people and cultures where they are practiced. Müller bases this conclusion largely on his experience of studying Indian religion in depth, as well as on his less detailed studies of other world religions.

Müller's caution concerning pathological assumption is important for us to remember today in the face of an atheist revival, sometimes called the "New Atheism." Adherents such as Richard Dawkins, Daniel Dennett, Sam Harris, and Christopher Hitchens begin with the assumption that the effects of religion are, overall, destructive to cultures and enervate individual personalities.[16] Some of these New Atheists are scientists and claim scientific evidence for their assertions. It turns out, however, that the globally available empirical evidence regarding the value of religion as a contributor to human flourishing shows exactly the opposite: although religion has been and still is

14. See Sigmund Freud, *The Future of an Illusion* (New York: Norton, 1927).

15. See Karl Marx and Friedrich Engels, *On Religion* (Moscow: Progress, 1957), for a collection of their writings on religious themes.

16. For a sampling of New Atheist work, see Richard Dawkins, *The God Delusion* (New York: Bantam, 2006); Daniel Dennett, *Breaking the Spell: Religion as a Natural Phenomenon* (New York: Penguin Books, 2007); Sam Harris, *The End of Faith: Religion, Terror, and the Future of Reason* (New York: Norton, 2005); Christopher Hitchens, *God Is Not Great: How Religion Poisons Everything* (New York: Twelve, 2007).

sometimes abused, its overall effect to both societies and individuals is overwhelmingly positive. By way of example, studies conducted by University of Texas sociologist Robert Woodberry show that cultures in which Christian mission workers have had significant influence are far better off than those that haven't experienced that influence.[17] In addition, the Heritage Foundation, a think tank based in Washington, DC, did a study of published works on the effects of religion on individuals—particularly in terms of their health. The analysis of over twenty published studies found, among other things, that religious people live longer, stay married longer, are happier, report lower levels of teen sexual activity, abuse drugs and alcohol less, contract infectious diseases with less frequency, and commit fewer acts of violent crime.[18]

What about *revealed religion*? The problem for Müller with making revealed religion the topic of scholarly endeavors is quite different from his problem with religion as pathology. Whereas Müller's bottom line with religion as pathology is that its assumption is not true to the facts, his problem with revealed religion is that the transcendent realm is not amenable to the methodologies of the humanities, social sciences, and/or natural sciences. The very point of transcendence is that it supersedes the mundane world we live in. As such it cannot be measured in the same way as material events that follow the laws of the natural world.

An additional reason that Müller cites for avoiding revealed religion as the focal point of religious study is that revelation leads to claims of uniqueness for one religion or another. As noted above, Müller was not at all opposed to Christian mission efforts—indeed, he saw his "science of religion" as a great boon to their work. And while it is unlikely that Müller would have opposed any religion's mission efforts, he did not want the study of natural religion to be in any way confused with the self-advocacies that these religious efforts entailed. Müller aspired to a separation between religious studies and theology.

17. See Robert Woodberry, "Missionary Roots of Liberal Democracy," *American Political Science Review* 106, no. 2 (2012): 244–74. See also the article on Woodberry's work: Andrea Palpant Dilley, "The Surprising Discovery about Those Colonialist, Proselytizing Missionaries," *Christianity Today*, January/February 2014, 34.

18. Study cited in the *National Catholic Reporter*, October 10–23, 2014, 3.

Müller would acknowledge, of course, that we study revealed religion indirectly when we observe what a belief in the transcendent on the part of religious adherents to a particular tradition does to their behavior. However, this type of study concerns the effects of such belief, not the belief itself or any possible substance behind the belief. Müller himself almost certainly believed in the transcendent God of Christianity, but his point was that we should bracket these beliefs when engaged in the scientific study of religion (a subject to which I will later return).

What is left for religious studies scholars is the study of *natural religion*—that is, religion as it can be observed in the behavior of individual human beings and their cultural groupings, including the values that motivate those cultures and the literature those cultures and religions produce. In the study of religion one should certainly acknowledge religious pathologies as they are discovered and allow for the possibility that religious truth is indeed transcendent in origin. However, the basic attitude of the religion scholar should be awe and respect in the face of what Müller calls "the greatest gift that God has bestowed on the children of man."[19] When studied with openness and objectivity, the history of religion as practiced by faithful human beings turns out to be a great gift indeed.

Why the Study of Religion Is Important

Ostensibly, it is not difficult to make a convincing case for the importance of engaging in the scholarly study of religion. Allow me to do that here by describing an assignment I regularly gave when I taught a course on religious pluralism at Austin Presbyterian Theological Seminary. As part of the assignment, which was called "Reading the Newspaper Religiously," I asked students to read two newspapers "religiously" during the course of our semester-long class. One newspaper needed to be a national newspaper, such as the *New York Times* or the *Washington Post*, and the other a local newspaper from Austin or the student's hometown. The students were asked to read every word of each newspaper cover to cover, and each week they were asked

19. Müller, *Chips from a German Workshop*, xxxii.

to write a report outlining the ways in which religion was mentioned in each newspaper. Not only did I ask them to pay special attention to global and local issues regarding religion, but I also asked them to pay special attention to the influence religion had on political, economic, social, and cultural events, both globally and locally.[20]

Without fail, the students were surprised at how frequently religion was mentioned throughout the papers; seldom was it confined to the Saturday afternoon religion page. Globally, I think they were startled to discover how often religion was a contributing cause of violent conflicts around the world. I especially remember one student's report on a story in the *New York Times* summarizing the violent conflicts taking place in the world at that particular time. The student expressed surprise at both the number of wars that were taking place (the author of the article counted forty-six and devoted a short, one-hundred-word paragraph describing each of them) and how often religion was mentioned as a significant factor in the conflict. Religion was mentioned in over half the articles and probably would have been mentioned more often if space had allowed. Some of these included Hindus and Muslims in India; Hindus and Sikhs in India; Christians, Muslims, and Jews in several different combinations in the Middle East; and Christians and Muslims in several sub-Saharan African countries. African Traditional Religion clashed with Christianity in South Africa, and the Russian Orthodox were at odds with the Ukrainian Catholics. Protestant Christians warred against Catholic Christians in Northern Ireland. The list went on and on.[21]

20. In the second half of the twentieth century, religion increasingly became a topic covered by secular journalists and television news reporters. The world incident that triggered this growing interest was the Iranian hostage crisis, an event that was incongruous to Western politicians and economists until Islamic religious beliefs were factored into the explanatory theses. After the crisis, religion was increasingly given its due as a motivating force in world news events. Print journalist Wes Pippert helped to organize religious news writers and other journalists interested in religion, and television documentary producer Bill Moyers said he thought religion was *the* story of the twenty-first century.

21. Although this article appeared in the early 1990s, it could be written today by adding several more theaters of conflict and making only minor changes to the details of the wars being fought. In all, only one or two deletions would need to be made. These types of conflicts never seem to end.

The student who wrote this particular report was astute enough to observe that most often it was not the religious institutions doing the fighting. Rather, it was the political leaders using religion as a supporting rationale for whatever conflict they were engaged in. But, truth be told, sometimes the religions *were* inciting the violence. The irony, the student rightly concluded, was that the very religions designed to promote peace and harmony and goodwill among all human beings were sometimes used for exactly the opposite purpose.

Other global challenges were noted, not all of them negative. Occasionally the religions did step up as peacemakers; conversations across religious lines seemed to be increasing. Furthermore, politicians seemed more sensitive to the idea that religious ideas do make a difference in public policy, and economists seemed more aware of the influence religion can have on marketing decisions. The bottom line? Anyone who is interested in understanding global affairs today ignores the role of religion at his or her peril.

The same is true of local affairs. Neighborhoods in the United States are no longer exclusively Christian;[22] the growth of the world religions in local communities is significant. Not only are mosques and temples appearing with regularity in the smallest of North American towns and cities, but public schools are also multireligious, making the determination of which religious holidays to observe problematic. A child's playmates may be Christian, but not necessarily. Military and hospital chaplains must be trained to provide religious services not just for Protestants, Catholics, and Jews, but also for Hindus, Buddhists, and Muslims. A whole host of interreligious issues arise on almost every level of American life today, and the more one knows about other religions, the easier the issues are to navigate.

Religious plurality is not a temporary issue. As the numbers of non-Christian adherents in our neighborhoods grow, so will their influence in determining public policy. There are already both Buddhist and Muslim members of the United States Congress, and state

22. See the study done by the Pew Forum on Religion and Public Life, "The Global Religious Landscape," 2010, Pew Research Center, http://www.pewforum.org/files/2014/01/global-religion-full.pdf, for details concerning the dramatic changes taking place in religious allegiances (or lack thereof) in the West.

and local political bodies are becoming similarly multireligious.[23] To be sure, the First Amendment of the US Constitution still guarantees freedom of religion, and the separation of church and state regulations means that religious influence on public policy cannot be overt. But indirect influences will continue to grow. Religious pluralism is no longer a theoretical issue to kick around in university classrooms, seminary seminars, and Sunday school class; it is part of the way we are living and will live in the future.

Religious surveys show that as much as 16 percent of the United States population claims no specific religious affiliation.[24] If these figures are accurate, this means that "no religious affiliation" is the fastest growing religious group in our culture today. Whether they go by atheists, nontheists, agnostics, or spiritual-but-not-religious, this group of people is practicing an implicit religion when measured by the Four-Question Definition. As such, they certainly merit the research of religious studies scholars.

The above discussion should make clear *why* we need to study religion, at least at a surface level, but it is possible to look at the challenge of religious studies in much more detail. If this introductory chapter has piqued the reader's interest in regard to the study of religion, then read on! The following chapters paint the rationale more fully, taking a closer look at how the nature of religion and religious adherence is changing in some fairly dramatic ways. Religion in our culture today is not the religion of our grandparents or even our parents. How and why religion is changing reveals an intriguing story—one we must all grapple with as we continue to study this most fascinating of human phenomena.

Scattered throughout this book are testimonies from religion scholars telling why they chose to study religion as an academic pursuit. It seems only fair that I add my testimony to the mix.

23. The first Muslim in the House of Representatives was Keith Ellison of Minnesota (elected in 2007); the first Hindu in the House was Tulsi Gabbard of Hawaii (elected in 2013); and the first Buddhist in the Senate was Mazie Hirono of Hawaii (also elected in 2013).

24. Pew Forum on Religion and Public Life, "Global Religious Landscape," 25.

Why I Study Religion

TERRY C. MUCK

I decided to study religion as I was finishing my master of divinity degree at Bethel Theological Seminary in St. Paul, Minnesota, in the spring of 1972. In the last year of my program at Bethel, it became clear to me that my gifts and calling did not lie in parish ministry. But where were my gifts and calling leading me?

I suspect many different people were wondering the same thing about where I was headed. While my professors surely didn't lose sleep over my vocational plans, they expressed concern and a willingness to help in my discernment. My parents thought I was going to become a pastor, and I'm sure this turn of events caused some worry. My wife, eager to quit work and start a family, braced herself for what she probably saw coming before I did—another graduate program, this time in the study of religion.

After applying to a number of PhD programs, I decided to enroll at Northwestern University in their comparative religion program. Students were asked to choose two different religions on which to focus their studies and write a comparative dissertation after completing the course work. I chose to study Christianity and Buddhism, and halfway through my course work I decided to write a dissertation on monasticism, comparing the teachings of the Buddhist Pali *Vinaya Pitaka* (the first and foremost Buddhist monastic rule) and St. Basil of Caesarea's *Longer and Shorter Rules* (the monastic rule at the root of many Eastern Orthodox Christian communities).

All these choices were good. The time I spent completing my doctorate program at Northwestern was an extremely happy period in my life. I loved everything about graduate study, and I loved the study of religion. From my first day on the Northwestern campus I felt at home. On the second day I had my first interview with my *doktorvater*, Edmund Perry. Knowing that I was a conservative Baptist evangelical, he attempted to put me at ease by lobbing me what he surely thought was an easy question: "What does John 1:1 mean when it comes to the study of non-Christian religions and ideologies?" I was nervous; I told him I didn't know.

But as day followed day and weeks became months, I gained confidence. I did well and ended my residency with a Fulbright-Hayes sponsored two-year field research trip to Sri Lanka, where I interviewed scores of Buddhist *bhikkhus* about their understanding of the *Vinaya Pitaka*. I gathered a great deal of data for my dissertation, but the experience of living in a Buddhist culture as a member of a minority religion probably did more to shape my study of religion than all the data in the world could provide.

I have asked myself why the life of a religion scholar fits me so well. I don't have a great answer. My cultural upbringing surely didn't encourage it. Neither my family life nor my religious tradition put religious studies on my radar. And as far as I know, a religious studies gene has not yet been discovered. I do remember that once I decided on graduate study after seminary, I chose religious studies based on an intuition of its importance for the global Christian church, much of which was still living with and operating by an outdated missiological approach to the other religions. I wanted to help change that. Mission, yes—triumphalism, no.

I have enjoyed a healthy dose of curiosity about other religions for as long as I can remember. Much to my mother's chagrin, I liked the visits of the Jehovah's Witnesses to our home; I even invited them back. I remember reading books about Tibetan Buddhism as a teenager. Even then, Buddhism was the most interesting of the world religions to me.

I'm sure that my need to understand why there are so many different religious traditions in the world was a factor in my choice. No one in my cultural upbringing had what I considered a satisfactory answer to religious diversity; in fact, I don't remember the question even being asked very often in those days.

I do know that meeting people of other religions and especially visiting their temples and mosques never failed to excite me. With perhaps the exception of baseball and baseball players, religions that are different from my own and religious people who believed differently than I do have always been intriguing to me.

Eventually, after graduate school, I embarked on a twenty-five year teaching career. All the things that I loved doing so much in graduate school—reading, writing, travel—I now got to do and was paid for doing it. I cannot think of a better way to have spent my life.

PART 1

WHY?

If you are a student taking your first course in religious studies, you need to know not only what it is you are studying and what skills you need as a student but also what benefits you will receive from such study. That's what the two chapters in part 1 aim to provide.

Chapter 1 begins by defining the study of religion. For this purpose, I use an essential definition—that is, an "x equals x" kind of definition. Following this I offer a brief history of the scholarly study of religion, which one might call a historical definition of the study of religion. I then look at the merchants, militarists, missionaries, and migrants who provided the essential data that the earliest scholars of religion used in this fledgling discipline. Finally, I examine some of the ways in which the study of religion is used in everyday life—its fruits, as one might say.

Chapter 2 suggests that the study of religion makes better world citizens, especially in terms of the ways in which they contribute to world peace, improve scholarship in religion, and (at least indirectly) improve religions by offering critical commentary from outside perspectives. Even though scholars are expected to be "objective" about their study, the chapter makes an argument that the student of religion will most likely experience a deeper understanding of his or her own religion in the process. Finally, since most readers of this book are probably Christians, I offer some thoughts on whether a "Christian" study of religion exists and what it might look like.

Maybe you are not a student taking your first course in religious studies. Maybe you have already taken quite a few such courses, or maybe you have developed sophisticated knowledge of religions in some other way, perhaps through a private course of reading or via study on the internet. If so, you will probably read chapters 1 and 2 differently, asking more sophisticated questions.

Chapter 1, for example, can be read as an exercise in definition, showing that any human phenomenon can be defined in many different ways. I use a number of these definitional strategies in the introduction and chapter 1, starting with a family resemblance definition for religion and moving, in turn, to an essential definition, a historical definition, and a personality-based definition for the study of religion. One might ask what other kinds of definitions could be put forward that are not used in this book. Metaphorical definitions come to mind here, particularly definitions that use metaphors and similes to explain what the study of religion is like. As an exercise, finish the following sentence: "The study of religion is like . . ." Any answer that is provided will be a metaphorical definition. As an additional exercise, brainstorm other ways in which the study of religion might be defined and explained.

Although chapter 2 introduces questions concerning the "objectivity" of the religious studies scholar, much more can be said about this subject, particularly about how a student's faith can either help or hinder his or her scholarly work. If you have already studied religion as an academic subject, you might reflect on the effects of that study on your personal religious commitments. Has it had little or no effect? Or has it had dramatic effect? As an exercise, consider writing five hundred words on the subject. You might also reflect in a more nuanced way on how you view objectivity, including (1) what scholarly objectivity is, (2) what scholarly objectivity is not, and (3) how scholarly objectivity might be attained.

When you have finished reading the two chapters that make up part 1, you should be able to define religion, define the study of religion, be aware of the history of religious studies, and know what skills are expected of someone who takes seriously the task of studying religion.

The two chapters in part 1 might also raise questions you wish to explore. Does the definition of religion change as the cultural influences of particular groups of people change? Although it is one thing to acknowledge that we cannot be totally objective in our study of religion, it is quite another to give up objectivity altogether, resulting in relativism. How might one inhabit the space between scholarly objectivity and skeptical relativism?

1

The Study of Religion

In the introduction I attempted to define *religion*. In this chapter I attempt to define the *study of religion*.

What is the study of religion? Defining the study of religion, it turns out, is almost as difficult as defining religion itself.[1] In the introduction to this book, I pointed out that *religion* can be defined differently, depending on the needs of the definer. Similarly, the *study of religion* can be defined differently, depending on the person who is doing the defining.[2] To use the language suggested by Max Müller in the last chapter, when religion's "cultured despisers"[3] (Sigmund Freud, Karl Marx, the New Atheists) define religion, they begin with the assumption that religion is pathological—something to be avoided. Thus the

1. For a further explication of this important topic, read the set of essays, "Study of Religion," in *The Encyclopedia of Religion*, ed. Mircea Eliade (New York: Macmillan, 1987), 14:64–92.

2. Morris Jastrow, in his classic *The Study of Religion* (London: Walter Scott, 1901), defines the study of religion as the gathering and systematic arrangement of data from all times and places, interpreted within a strictly naturalistic human framework. Within this framework, the inner, emotional aspects of the data are explored and a comparative study is carried out to discover the essential laws of the development of religion.

3. "Cultured despisers" was coined by Friedrich Schleiermacher (1768–1834) to describe Enlightenment thinkers whose project included supplanting religious authority with the authority of human reason.

study of such religion is seen as something roughly comparable to the medical diagnosis of a disease. On the contrary, when the adherents of different religions (such as Buddhists, Christians, Hindus, or Muslims) define religion, they are likely to define it as revealed from God or the transcendent as they understand it, so the study of religion turns out to be something akin to theology, Vedology, or Buddhology. Without suggesting that either one of these ways of studying religion is necessarily wrong, Müller advocates approaching religious phenomenon scientifically and objectively. Rather than considering all religion bad or privileging one religion over all the others, Müller thought that we should learn to study religion as human phenomena; thus began the development of the discipline we now call "religious studies." With that in mind, I will proceed in this chapter to answer the following question: *How do we define what religious studies scholars do when they "study religion"?*

Like any terminology requiring a definition, the study of religion can be defined functionally, essentially, and/or historically. In the introduction to this book, I gave an example of a functional definition (sometimes called a "family resemblance definition"), which I call the Four-Question Definition of religion. For my discussion on the study of religion, I will use an essential definition:

> The modern, scholarly study of religion is the comprehensive study of religion and religions as human phenomena using both historical and systematic methodologies, as far as possible without dogmatic presuppositions, comparing and contrasting both universal and particular features of those religions.[4]

What is the difference between a functional definition and an essential one? While a functional definition emphasizes the uses to which religion is put by its adherents, an essential definition attempts to define religion by what it is. Most dictionary definitions of nouns (like religion or the study of religion) are essential definitions. Such

---

4. This is my definition. When compared with the elements that Morris Jastrow thought should be included in a definition of the study of religion (see footnote 2 in this chapter), my definition incorporates roughly the same criteria, although phrased differently, which perhaps reflects over one hundred years of religious studies history.

definitions explicitly state the characteristics of the noun under discussion and by implication eliminate the noun from the categories of
things that are not stated. A dictionary usually states that in order to
be a "study of religion," a phenomenon must include characteristic
A, characteristic B, characteristic C, and so on. For example, in my
definition of the study of religion, characteristic A is "human phenomena," as the subject of such study; characteristic B is "historical and
systematic methodologies," which are used in the study of religion;
and characteristic C is to do such study without "dogmatic presuppositions." For an activity to be considered a "study of religion," it
must include all three characteristics: A, B, and C.

Scientists love essential definitions. They are precise. They set
specific rubrics for measuring things. The great strength of essential
definitions is that anyone anywhere can use such a definition to either
include or exclude a specific human behavior as religious—or not. In
the case of this chapter, an essential definition of the study of religion
can help teach us what the study of religion is about—and what, if
anything, it is not about.

A Historical Definition of the Study of Religion

A functional definition defines something by what it does. An essential definition defines something by what it is and is not. A historical
definition defines something by how it has existed in historical time:
how it began, how it developed, and what it is today as a result of
that history. Let us turn now to an extended historical definition of
the study of religion. How did the modern, scholarly study of religion
begin and develop?[5]

---

5. To be clear about the differences between these kinds of definitions, let's define
the religion Christianity. A historical definition involves a summary of the narrative:
"Christianity is the religion founded by Jesus Christ, who lived from 5 BCE to 29 CE,
and promoted by Jesus's twelve disciples and numerous theologians and church leaders in the years that followed." An essentialist definition might read: "Christianity is
religious belief that includes all the elements of the Apostles' Creed." And a functional
(or family resemblance) definition might go something like this: "Christianity is a
human religion that functions for its adherents much like Hinduism functions for
most residents of India and Confucianism for most Chinese. It provides answers to
life's ultimate questions: Who am I? Why am I here? Where am I going?"

The study of religion as a Western academic subject is a relatively new discipline. Prior to the mid-nineteenth century, studying "religion" usually meant that the subject matter was one's own religion, with occasional thoughts on how other religions compared with it. The study of religion, in other words, was nearly synonymous with theology. In the mid-nineteenth century, several trends gave these occasional and dogmatic thoughts about other religions a new, distinctive character. One trend, ironically, was the Christian mission movement. After several centuries of development, its practitioners were able to supply Western scholars with a wealth of material on non-Christian religions. A second trend at this same time was anthropologists and archaeologists who were studying non-Western cultures and sending back an avalanche of data on cultural and religious practices in Asia, Africa, and Micronesia. The third trend involved the flowering of an intellectual approach to interpreting data that emphasizes human rationality rather than divine agency. This Enlightenment viewpoint was tailor-made for attempts to make some sense of this body of religious information.

The early science of religion produced scholarly works of two types. The first is typified by the work of a man whom I have already introduced and who is often called the father of religious studies: Max Müller (1823–1900).[6] Using data obtained through his linguistic studies, Müller traced the history of religious systems and then wrote comparative studies that made religion itself, rather than a specific religion, the underlying category of study. The second type of scholarship is typified by the work of James George Frazer (1854–1941), who took the catalog approach to making sense of this deluge of religious information. His twelve-volume *Golden Bough* is organized according to cross-religious categories such as magic, taboo, and totemism, with religious data from different religious traditions filed under the appropriate heading.[7]

One can see in Müller's work the influence of the scientific model. The task of the scientist of religion was to gather as much data

6. See Nirad Chaudhuri's biography, *Scholar Extraordinary: The Life of Friedrich Max Müller* (London: Chatto & Windus, 1974).

7. Probably the best way to get a handle on Frazer's massive work is to read the one-volume abridgement of *The Golden Bough*, which was prepared by Frazer and his wife, Lady Frazer (New York: Macmillan, 1922).

as possible and then construct theories that attempted to explain the data in wider and wider circles of inclusivity. The goal was not the discovery of metaphysical truth but the accurate description of meaningful religious phenomena of the world in which we live. Given this reliance on the scientific model (in an attempt to distinguish this method of study from theology), it is not surprising to find that when the prevailing scientific theory of the nineteenth century changed, the study of comparative religion also began to change.

In some ways, Charles Darwin's theory of evolution was a godsend for comparative religionists. By making it scientifically respectable to offer secular explanations for human phenomena, evolutionism opened a new arena of activity for the fledgling science of religion.[8] Divine intervention, which was a staple of most premodern explanatory theses of religion, was no longer needed as a way to explain why things happen as they do.

Sociologists, psychologists, and philosophers quickly filled this new arena with substantial explanatory theses that attempted globally to describe the origins and development of all religion in comprehensive schemata. The great sociologists of religion, Émile Durkheim (1858–1917)[9] and Max Weber (1864–1920),[10] wrote extensively in this arena, and a uniquely American contribution to the discipline was offered by the psychologists of religion, headed by William James (1842–1910) and his *Varieties of Religious Experience*.[11] Perhaps more than any other, the philosophers of religion began to produce systematic philosophies of the development of religious consciousness, such as that by Pierre Teilhard de Chardin (1881–1955).[12]

This ferment of scholarly activity in kindred disciplines encouraged the carving out of methodologies designed specifically for the study

8. Charles Darwin, *Origin of the Species* (New York: Signet, 2003).
9. See esp. Émile Durkheim, *The Elementary Forms of the Religious Life* (New York: Free Press, 1995).
10. The best introduction to Max Weber's work is his *The Protestant Ethic and the Spirit of Capitalism* (New York: Penguin Books, 2002).
11. William James, *The Varieties of Religious Experience* (Mineola, NY: Dover, 2002).
12. De Chardin's two major works in which his understanding of religious consciousness is developed are *The Phenomenon of Man* (New York: Harper, 1961) and *The Divine Milieu* (New York: Perennial, 2001).

STUDY AID

THE RELIGIOUS STUDIES FAMILY TREE

The scholarly study of religion follows a different periodization than some other scholarly disciplines. The elements of the periodization are common (premodern, modern, postmodern), but religious studies has a very long "premodern" period and a very short "postmodern" period. Like most such disciplinary histories, all three periods continue to influence today's study of religion.

PREMODERN (UP UNTIL 1850). For premoderns, religion was/is little differentiated from the rest of life. Because of this, its "study" was coterminous with tribal history, including politics, economics, and cultural life. Most studies of religion during this period were merely the study of one's own "tribal" religion, what we would today call theology.

When premodern manifestations of religion are studied today, the best methodologies are those of the archaeologists (since some of these religions are ancient) and anthropologists (since one goal of anthropology is to consider social groups in their entirety).

TRANSITIONS. The transition to the modern period can be helpfully illustrated by three global meetings:

Parliament of World Religions (Chicago, 1893): This meeting is sometimes considered the first gathering of religious leaders from around the world. It is often pointed to as the event that initiated formal religious dialogue as a way for Christians to relate to people of other faiths.

International Association for the History of Religion (Paris, 1900): This was the first of twenty such gatherings, held roughly every five years. Some scholars refer to this meeting as the first to focus on the academic study of religion.

of religion. Objective histories of particular religious traditions began to appear from scholars like Nathan Söderblom (1886–1931) and William Brede Kristensen (1867–1953). Other scholars, in the cataloging tradition of James George Frazer, adapted a methodology loosely related to Edmund Husserl's philosophical phenomenology and began to develop cross-religious categories in order to better compare and contrast religious traditions. Gerardus van der Leeuw (1890–1950) and Rudolf Otto (1869–1937) published works in what came to be called the phenomenology of religion tradition, which relied on a method that advocated a temporary suspension (or bracketing) of one's own beliefs (*epoche*) in order to clearly identify the unique character of

World Missionary Conference (Edinburgh, 1910): This conference is seen by some as the culmination of the nineteenth-century Protestant mission movement and by others as the beginning of the twentieth-century ecumenical movement. It is best seen as both—after this meeting, Christian mission changed.

MODERN (1850–2000). The so-called modern scholars of religion saw the need for descriptions of religion that were somehow distinguished from theological descriptions that served in-house communities of faith well but did little to consider religion as a generic category of human existence.

Max Müller and James George Frazer are regarded as the founders of religious studies. The following list includes the disciplines that have contributed to religious studies:

Psychology: William James, Sigmund Freud, Carl Gustav Jung
Social sciences: sociology (Émile Durkheim, Max Weber); anthropology (E. B. Tylor, Wilhelm Schmidt)
Biblical studies: Julius Wellhausen, William Robertson Smith
Philosophy: Pierre Teilhard de Chardin, Rudolf Otto
Religious studies proper: Nathan Söderblom, Gerardus van der Leeuw, Joachim Wach

POSTMODERN (2000–PRESENT). The postmodern period represents the dawning awareness on religious studies scholars of the situatedness of all knowledge, depending on time (history) and place (context).

Based on Jean Jacques Waardenburg, *Classical Approaches to the Study of Religion*, vol. 3 (The Hague: Mouton, 1973–74).

religious phenomena (*sui generis*); the goal of this method was simply to understand (*verstehen*) the religion. These two approaches to the collection of the data of religious studies—the longitudinal, historical study and the cross-sectional, phenomenological study—have been dominant methodologies in comparative religion ever since.[13]

In other ways, Darwin's theory of evolution sent the discipline of religious studies down a dead-end road. The search for a common

13. Both James George Frazer's *Golden Bough* and Gerardus van der Leeuw's *Religion in Essence and Manifestation*, 2 vols., trans. J. E. Turner (1938; repr., New York: Harper & Row, 1963) are works of phenomenology, whereas works like Weber's *Protestant Ethic and the Spirit of Capitalism* are historical in approach.

origin and developmental pattern to all religion proved to be a remarkably contentious and ultimately frustrating enterprise because the
data of religions from around the world showed itself to be extremely
elastic when it came to shaping theories. Some of the developmental
schemes posited that all religions come from animistic roots, invest-
ing all being with spiritual power and moving all religions toward a
more well-defined polytheism that eventually became part of the great
monotheistic religious traditions. Other developmental schemes took
roughly the same material and generated theories that posited exactly
the opposite. These theories posited high gods—monotheisms that
over time devolved into polytheistic and then spiritist religions, with
more and more layers of gods between humans and the high gods. As
more and more of the world's religious systems were studied, they
were found to be less and less amenable to universal, step-by-step
developmental patterns.

In most academic circles, the recognition that these essentially
Western-based universal categories and developmental patterns do
not necessarily fit within other cultures led to a kind of cultural
relativism, which argued that generalizations cannot be made from
culture to culture. Each religion must be studied on its own terms.
This move matched some of the insights phenomenologists had made
regarding the subjectivity of the religious scholar him- or herself but
went beyond these insights by suggesting that the suspension of one's
point of view might be a chimera that extended not only to cultures
but also to cultural observers. As a result, many scholars began to
see cultural relativism as a dead end (similar to the one faced by evo-
lutionists), making any kind of cross-cultural (and cross-religious)
communication nearly impossible.

This turn of events brought about two methodological "middle
roads" between the metaphysical universalism of historical evolutionism and the radical particularism of phenomenology. The first came
to be called *functionalism*,[14] a view that finds the core of religion in
the roles it plays in addressing personal and societal needs rather
than in truth-claims of the gods, of the gods' representatives, or in

14. Durkheim is the classic functionalist, who sees religion largely as a phenomenon
performing distinct functions in society.

the unconnected, conditioned realities of discrete cultures. While the needs that functionalists identify as "religious" vary, all functionalists hold that "religion is as religion does." Functionalist theories of religion are among the most widely used in religious studies today and in one sense may be seen as extensions of Durkheim's pioneering work. Moreover, the methodology is particularly useful to sociologists of religion, such as Joachim Wach (1898–1955) and Robert Bellah (1927–2013), and anthropologists Mary Douglas (1921–2007) and Clifford Geertz (1926–2006).

A second middle road between universalism and particularism is structuralism. Rooted in the work of linguist Ferdinand de Saussure (1857–1913) and given methodological form by social anthropologist Claude Levi-Strauss (1908–2009), structuralists see the use of language and language systems as the mediator between universals and particulars. Religions and cultures came to be viewed as analogous to languages. Each language (or religion) has its own vocabulary and grammatical rules. However, each language (or religion) also has structural features in common that seem to span all languages or religions. Structuralists claim that these features allow people of one religious tradition to recognize themselves in another person's religious tradition. The otherness of that tradition is maintained, however, because those features' full meaning resides more in the holistic pattern of that religious tradition than in the content of a particular belief. The recognition of these common structural features allows empathy that may lead to accurate knowledge of the other, but not necessarily to full understanding of it. Structuralism is on the cutting edge of approaches to religion that are being explored by scholars today. History of religions and phenomenological methodologies still provide much of the on-the-ground content and data of religious studies, but that data is increasingly filtered through the lens of structuralist forms.

The Study of Religion as Defined by the People Who Contributed

Modern scholars of religion owe a debt of gratitude to several different kinds of people—merchants, militarists, missionaries, and migrants—who, knowingly or unknowingly, were instrumental to the development of the study of religion. Some of these people contributed by simply meeting others who practiced different religions and learning about them in the same way that one learns about any new acquaintances—by observing what they do and listening to what they say. Some of these contributors became so intrigued by what they saw and heard that they began to more intentionally amass data about religions other than their own. Some began to seek out firsthand acquaintances with people of other religions in order to ascertain what they believed—that is, they initiated contacts in order to champion their own religion.

Merchants

A common way for religions to spread is as a result of trade activity among cultures. Often the traders themselves unintentionally contribute to the spread of their religion by simply practicing their own religion. Alternatively, more mission-minded folks might use the economic vehicle of trade as a way to hitch a ride to a new place of witness. In other words, a missionary voyages to a foreign country on a ship that is primarily focused on trading economic goods from one country to another. The following two examples illustrate how merchant activity has contributed to the spread of Christianity.

The Silk Road included a set of overland trading routes that extended from China to the Middle East.[15] The three primary routes consisted of a northern route, a southern route, and a route in between the two. These trading routes were called the Silk Road because merchants in South Asia, Central Europe, and the Middle East were willing to trade their goods (including herbs and spices) for the silk offered by the merchants residing in East Asia (primarily China). In many cases, gold was used to pay for Chinese silk, particularly during the days of the Roman Empire. In the process of these trades, religions were also exchanged. The Chinese merchants were Confucianists and Taoists, while many from India were Hindu and, after the first century, Buddhist. Greek traders often knew about Judaism and Christianity, and in the seventh century Arab traders brought their Islamic culture with them.

15. Liu Xinru, *The Silk Road in World History* (New York: Oxford University Press, 2010).

The second example of merchants who helped in the discovery and understanding of non-Christian religions involves the British East India Company,[16] the success of which contributed to the growth and development of the mighty British Empire. Although originally the East India Company would not allow Christian missionaries to travel with them to South and East Asia, they eventually did. As spices and exotic goods were traded with Indonesia and other Southeast Asian islands, the Christian religion spread. The groundwork for the nineteenth-century spread of Christianity, sometimes called the Great Age of Missionaries, was undoubtedly laid by the contacts the British East India Company developed with other cultures.

Militarists

Religions have also been introduced and spread by warfare. Military conquerors not only get to write definitive histories, but also get to determine religious adherence. History is replete with examples of militarists imposing their religion on the peoples they conquered. Oftentimes this imposition was fairly benign—that is, it was not a requirement that the conquered peoples join the religion of their conquerors. That the conquerors were able to defeat the indigenous peoples was often explained in terms of their god(s) being more powerful than the god(s) of those they subjugated. Without doubt, the great Greek leader Alexander the Great (356–323 BCE)[17] spread Greek philosophy and religion near and far on his path from the Middle East to India, but he did so largely through conversation and modeling. A more recent example is the early British East India Company, which did not allow Christian missionaries in the lands they entered (a pattern that eventually changed).

However, the influence of military leaders on religion has not always been benign. Military conquerors often demanded conversion to their religion on the part of the people they defeated, such

16. Robert Brenner, *Merchants and Revolution: Commercial Change, Political Conflict, and London's Overseas Traders* (Princeton: Princeton University Press, 1993).

17. See *Alexander the Great: The Brief Life and Towering Exploits of History's Greatest Conqueror as Told by His Original Biographers*, ed. Tania Gergel (New York: Penguin Books, 2004).

as the early Christian militarists from Spain and Portugal who commanded the indigenous peoples of the Americas to join their religion on pain of death. The most recent example of conversion by the sword is the Islamic movement—both from the Middle East across North Africa to Europe, and also from the Middle East across South Asia to India and on to Indonesia. While conversion is sometimes demanded on pain of death, at other times people who choose not to acknowledge Allah and his prophet Muhammad are reduced to second-class citizens because of their refusal to swear obedience to the Islamic cause.

Missionaries

The most explicit way in which religions have become known and spread to nonadherents is through intentional missionary effort. Among the religions, mission methods vary in both intensity and means. The most energetic missionary religions have been Buddhism, Christianity, and Islam.[18] The founders of these three religions— Gautama, Jesus, and Muhammad—each gave an explicit charge to their followers to spread the dharma, gospel, and Qur'an worldwide. As a result, Christianity and Islam have grown to be the two largest religions in the world, and Buddhism has spread worldwide from its base in India, with a significant presence in the West.

Other religions—Hinduism and Judaism come to mind—have a more muted approach to missions. Historically, both have eschewed mission methods aimed at conversion, although pockets of both Hindus and Jews do actively seek converts. In spite of this disavowal, however, both religions have spread significantly, although neither has had particular numerical success outside their geographic origins. Jews, for example, live in many countries of the world, but

18. As an interesting study in contrasts, consider the following approaches: in a book written from the point of view of a Christian theology of religion, this discussion would be called a study of Christian mission; in a religious studies textbook (like the one you are now reading), the discussion would be about the spread of religions. Mission is a theological category of thought, and the geographical spread of a religion and its institutions is a sociological category (used in religious studies). In sociology, the spread of religion is also called *diffusion*. See Robert L. Montgomery, *The Spread of Religions* (Hackensack, NJ: Long Dash, 2007).

their numbers aren't substantial outside the Middle East and the United States.

It may be that in our early twenty-first-century world it is almost impossible for any religion not to be missionary in some sense. The presence of social media makes direct observation of religion easy, and as any good missioner will tell you, being seen and acknowledged is the first step toward good mission work. A number of years ago several students of mine were writing doctoral dissertations on Korean shamanism and its early influence on Christianity in Korea. I knew only a little about shamanism. To address this lack, I read the normative literature, but I also discovered that on YouTube I could observe Korean shamanistic ritual services and listen to interviews with shaman leaders in that country. Almost any religion in the world today can be accessed in the same way.

Migrants

An observant reader might notice that the first three categories of people who spread their religion—merchants, militarists, missionaries—are often mixed. Missionaries accompany armies, not necessarily to do mission work but to service the members of the armed forces. Some merchants may be bivocational, having both a business and an avocation (a sideline interest or hobby) of missions. In a similar way, the fourth category of migrants is a mixed bag.[19] Obviously, large migrant populations take their religious traditions with them, becoming (at least) inadvertent missionaries as they move from country to country. Sometimes, however, people migrate in search of religious freedom. The European migrants who came to North America from the fifteenth century onward were often searching for a place to practice their religion more freely.[20]

It is probably safe to say that people today migrate from one place to another, either freely or forcibly, for largely economic reasons. They

19. Studies of migrants today are often bunched under a research agenda called "diaspora studies." See Stephane Dufoix, *Diasporas* (Berkeley: University of California Press, 2008) for an introduction.

20. For an introduction to the effects of migrants on religion, see John Hinnells, "The Study of Diaspora Religion," in *A New Handbook of Living Religions*, ed. John Hinnells (Oxford: Blackwell, 1997), 682–89.

STUDY AID

THE CHINESE DIASPORA

Approximately fifty million Chinese live outside China. One nation-state, Singapore, has a majority Chinese population—almost three million Chinese live in Singapore. Ten other countries have Chinese populations over one million.

Thailand: 9.3 million
Indonesia: 8.8 million
Malaysia: 7 million
United States: 3.8 million
Burma: 1.6 million
Canada: 1.4 million
Peru: 1.3 million
Philippines: 1.2 million
Vietnam: 1 million
Russia: 1 million

From Terry Muck, Harold Netland, and Gerald McDermott, eds., *Handbook of Religion* (Grand Rapids: Baker Academic, 2014), 238.

may be searching for better opportunities or fleeing from abysmal economic conditions. In 2013, estimates placed the number of world-wide immigrants at about 232 million people.[21] If one assumes that migrating people take their religions with them (a safe assumption), then it is clear that religion spreads through migration.

Clearly, all four groups of people—merchants, militarists, missionaries, and migrants—contributed data and method to the developing study of religion. While not all the data was reliable and not all the methods used in their "studies" would pass muster in the halls of academia, the discipline of study known today as religious studies was mined from the raw ore of these early observers.

The Uses of the Scholarly Study of Religion

Academics of any discipline are fond of saying that the information and data produced by their scholarly endeavors are an end in

21. United Nations, *Trends in International Migrant Stock* (New York: United Nations, 2013).

themselves—and there is much truth to that statement. But religion scholars will, if pressed, also tell you of the many secondary benefits of the study of religion. Three examples follow.

The Study of Religion Informs Publics

Much of what is produced in the office of the religious studies scholar has real value in informing various publics about the nature of religions that so obviously inform day-to-day and year-to-year events in the world and cultures in which we live. That influence can be positive, but it can also be negative.[22] The religions of the world contribute to both our well-being and our angst. While the religion scholar is not tasked with making a judgment concerning whether a particular religion is good or bad, he or she is obligated to provide the information and data that will help others decide that question.

One of the most productive religion scholars in this realm is sociologist of religion Rodney Stark, who teaches at Baylor University. At last count Stark had written over thirty-five books of reliable information, data, and theory about the sociological effects of religion. One of these, *The Rise of Christianity*, was nominated for a Pulitzer Prize.[23] Stark's work has not always been popular—in part because he does not shy away from relating data that may skewer the sacred cows of the sociology of religion. But he reports it all the same. Stark relates the following about his beginnings as a student of religion:

> I began doing the sociology of religion initially as a matter of coincidence and continued because I found the field to be so incredibly underdeveloped as to provide endless opportunities. In my first semester of graduate school at Berkeley I was enrolled in the required methods course and one of the two instructors was Charles Y. Glock. I had arrived without any financial support and was continuing to work nights covering the police for the *Oakland Tribune*. The midterm exam was a disaster—a mean of less than 50 percent (more than 100 students) and the second highest grade was 82 percent. I got 95 percent

22. Consider, e.g., the controversy that erupted when the public learned that the US Central Intelligence Agency was recruiting scholarly anthropologists to help the agency with its assessments of foreign cultures and peoples.

23. Rodney Stark, *The Rise of Christianity* (San Francisco: HarperCollins, 1996).

and was immediately hired by Glock as his research assistant to work on a study of religion and anti-Semitism. He was so busy as director of the Survey Research Center that I was able to take over the study and soon he gave me total freedom—with the result being four books. Along the way I discovered that the ancestors of the field—Weber, Durkheim, and Marx—were of little value and that the field needed to be restarted from scratch. I quickly became absorbed in the many lovely puzzles it posed, and am still at it—my 34th and 35th books appeared in 2014: one of them being *Religious Hostility: A Global Assessment of Hatred and Terror*.[24]

The Study of Religion Contributes to Human Solidarity and World Peace

As the reader will see from the "Why I Study Religion" features scattered throughout this book, religion scholars often choose to study religion because they want to use their scholarship as a force for good: for relieving poverty, for increasing justice, for creating conditions of peace among the religious peoples of the world. The study of religion produces understanding, and understanding helps to bring about fellowship and friendship; in turn, fellowship and friendship lead to reconciliation of groups of people and individuals.

Rosemary Radford Ruether has labored mightily to show the value of studying religion in order to more fully understand social conditions around the world.[25] She has been an unfailing champion of women, the poor, disadvantaged minorities, and others in their quests to overcome prejudice, exclusion, disease, malnutrition, and injustice. Ruether currently teaches at the Claremont School of Theology, and she relates the following about her start in the study of religion:

> In 1952–54 I was the editor of our high school newspaper. We prided ourselves in having articles on the whole range of issues, but I often wrote on the religious dimension of issues, as a way of addressing their deeper meaning. When I graduated from high school in 1954 I was appointed to give the commencement address on the meaning of

---

24. Rodney Stark, email to author, October 14, 2013.
25. Ruether has written many books. *Sexism and God Talk* (Boston: Beacon, 1993) is a good introduction to her important body of work.

"religion." The creative writing class was assigned to write these addresses which I and others were to "give." But I didn't like the address they had written, which seemed to reflect a narrow, sectarian view of religion. I insisted on writing my own. This created a crisis with the creative writing class. The faculty resolved the issue by having me read both addresses before a faculty committee who would decide which was better, without knowing which one was written by whom. They unanimously picked the one I had written as the better essay. I felt vindicated in my vision!

I went to college at Scripps College in Claremont, 1954–58. In their humanities curriculum, religion was integrated within the fullness of humanistic education. Toward the end of my college work, I read an appeal by a local science department to study science. It was couched in a way that dismissed religion and humanistic thought as meaningless, "unscientific." I was shocked. This confirmed my decision to study religion more fully. I did a master's degree in Early Christianity and went on for a PhD in the history of Christian thought. I have been writing and teaching on religion ever since, mainly in theological seminaries attached to universities. I have never thought of my work in religion as separate from humanistic, social, economic and political thought, but rather as a way of integrating everything together in the quest for deeper meaning.[26]

The Study of Religion Sharpens Personal Religious Belief and Practice

There are significant existential benefits from engaging in the scholarly study of religion. The most universal and, ironically, the least talked about is the "iron sharpens iron" phenomenon. When a scholar studies another religion, he or she learns a great deal of additional information about his or her own religion. Comparison, as we shall see later in this book, is an unavoidable human exercise and an essential part of rationality. When one studies another religion, comparison inevitably takes place with one's own religion. The effects of this comparison tend to sharpen one's understanding of both religions.

Larry Poston, professor of religion at Nyack College, came to the study of religion as a result of an existential moment in his life. When

26. Rosemary Radford Ruether, email to author, October 25, 2013.

he realized that he could not be religious in the way he felt called to be religious unless he more fully understood the way in which other religions came in contact with his own, he enrolled in a program of religious studies and eventually made teaching religion his career. Poston summarizes his own process in this way:

> My initial interest in comparative religion arose during my graduate studies in missiology at Trinity Evangelical Divinity School. Adopting the exclusivistic soteriology of historic Christianity meant that I would have to contend with the competing truth claims of the world's religions. To me it seemed that evangelicals were particularly unprepared for such encounters, having pursued a "plow them under" approach for centuries. But the history of missions made it clear that such a philosophy of ministry was singularly ineffective; while Christian missionaries had been relatively successful with primal religionists, they had failed almost completely with the world-class faith systems. The challenge of these facts led me to Eric Sharpe's *Comparative Religion: A History*, which introduced me to Max Müller's credo "He who knows one, knows none." Convinced of the truth of this statement, I began formal study of the religions at the University of Gothenburg while on assignment to teach at the Nordic Bible Institute in Sweden. Contact in that country with Muslim refugees from the Middle East confirmed the challenge involved in missionary work among the adherents of Islam, and such experiences enhanced my desire to acquire expertise in the various religions in order better to contextualize the Christian message.[27]

The elephant in the room thus far is the relationship between the personal religious beliefs of a scholar of religion and his or her scholarship. Can one be a Buddhist confessionally and study religion objectively? Can one be a champion of the value of religious studies and its methods and at the same time be a champion of Christianity? Is it possible to fully submit to the truths of the Qur'an and make good use of these different approaches to the study of religion? The answer I argue for in the next chapter is yes, though I qualify it by one

27. Larry Poston, email to author, October 18, 2013.

caveat: the methods of religious studies work for people committed to their own religions so long as the methods are seen as *useful tools* in gathering and handling data of a very specific nature and not as *normative methodologies* over against theological and revelatory ones. Theories of religion become problematic for Christians, Buddhists, Muslims, Hindus, and others only when those theories begin to claim for themselves absolute status, replacing propositional and ethical absolutes with methodological ones.

But that short answer is not enough. What kind of positive statement about a religious approach to the study of religion can be made? That is, who is the ideal student of religion and what skills does he or she need in order to be a proficient religious studies scholar?

Why I Study Religion

MARK JUERGENSMEYER, UNIVERSITY OF CALIFORNIA, SANTA BARBARA

Why I chose to study religion is a less interesting story than why I chose to study religious violence. Religion is in my family's veins. I was raised in a pious Protestant family in the rural Midwest, and the church—believe it or not—was the most socially progressive community in town. So I went to seminary in New York City and studied with Reinhold Niebuhr, who taught me that religion is about politics and social life. I discovered this same truth on my own as a rebellious political activist in the civil rights and antiwar movements of the 1960s; part of my motivation was a religious conviction to help bring about a just and peaceful world. In India, I found a whole country full of religion and politics, which became my arena of intellectual exploration.

But why would a nice guy from Southern Illinois—a Christian pacifist and a Gandhian—turn to the study of religious violence? The answer is the Sikhs. I lived for a couple of years in the Punjab, the region in the far north of the country in the Himalayan foothills, where the largest religious community was not Hindu or Muslim but a relatively new religious tradition that followed a series of spiritual masters from the sixteenth and seventeenth centuries. What attracted me to Sikhism was not only its peaceful spiritual teaching but also the egalitarian spirit of the community. Sikhs are warm, generous, openhearted rural people, and I found in them a certain kinship.

When an awful spiral of violence began to emerge in the Punjab in the 1980s between the Indian government and rural Sikh youth, I wanted to know why. Why was this movement violent, and why was it religious? The questions were not only close to my academic subject of interest in religion and politics but also close to my heart. I wanted to know how people from the Sikh community whom I so loved and respected could be engaged in clashes so brutal and vicious. I wanted to know why religion—the harbinger of peace—could be suffused with blood and conflict.

After the tragic invasion of the Sikh's Golden Temple in 1984, I returned to the Punjab with questions. I interviewed followers of the fallen leader of the Sikh uprising, Sant Jarnail Singh Bhindranwale, and listened to recordings of his sermons. What I discovered propelled me through many of my comparative studies of religious activism around the world in the several decades since. I found that Bhindranwale and his movement saw the political world through religious eyes. They understood the mundane clashes of the material world to be a part of a grand unfolding drama, a scenario of cosmic war. Their politics were part of a religious tableau.

As a result, my studies of particular instances of religious violence have led me back to where I started: trying to understand the role that religious ideas and images play in the human imagination and in the aspirations of social life. I have also learned that the best way—the basic way, really—to study religious phenomena is to go inside them, to try to understand them from the perspective of the believer. This means taking seriously the notion that religion portrays "an alternative reality," as Robert Bellah put it in his last book, *Religion in Human Evolution.* To enter into the religious imagination, I have found, is not only a sound intellectual procedure but also a way of entering into aspects of humanity's complex sociospiritual world. It is a window into the hidden recesses of our selves.

2

The Student of Religion

Students who choose to study religion come in all sizes and shapes. Some take one course out of curiosity and never take another. For others, the first course is just the beginning of a lifelong interest that can lead to several levels of commitment, ranging from religious studies as an avocation to the study and teaching of religion as a vocation. Students who enroll in a religious studies course for the first time begin a journey of discovery, a journey that is as much about the student as it is about the study of religion.

Thus I am writing this chapter on the student of religion, aware that you may be anywhere along this spectrum of interest, which ranges from curiosity to vocational commitment. While you may already know where you fall on that spectrum, it's more likely you don't. Like a first course in a progressive dinner of many courses, you will wait to see whether the first course tastes good enough to encourage you to continue eating. For some a "snack" might be enough; others will want the full meal.

How will you make that decision? Many factors will intervene, some of them quite personal and having little to do with the study of religion. Other factors will be integral to the nature of this particular form of scholarship. The study of religion seems to suit students with a particular set of traits—traits that students either possess at the beginning of their study or develop along the way. In this chapter I have chosen to deal with three traits that I think are particularly important for the scholar of religion: objectivity/empathy, scholarship, and religiosity. These three traits overlap, as can be seen in the discussion below, but I try to discuss them separately.

Let me begin by introducing a helpful guide in this exploration: Joachim Wach (1898–1955). Wach was a pivotal scholar of religion who has a great deal to say about the benefits a scholar of religion receives from his or her study as well as the skills and aptitudes such scholarship requires.[1] Wach was a German scholar of religion who began his teaching career at the University of Leipzig. His family was Jewish, descended from the famous German philosopher Moses Mendelsohn. Even though Wach and his family had converted to Lutheranism several generations prior, the Nazi government forced him from his professorship at Leipzig because of his Jewish ancestry. Wach emigrated to the United States, where he got a position at Brown University and taught from 1935 to 1944. He moved on to teach at the University of Chicago in 1945. At Chicago, Wach quickly became head of the History of Religion faculty, a group of scholars who achieved fame as the Chicago School of the study of religion.[2] He died of a heart attack in 1955.

Wach's contributions to the scholarship of religion were key to the establishment and growth of the discipline in the United States. He wrote many books in both the history of religion and the sociology of religion, doing much to establish each area of study in the Western halls of academia. His books include *Introduction to the History of Religions*, *Sociology of Religion*, *Types of Religious Experience: Christian and Non-Christian*, and *The Comparative Study*

1. Joseph Kitagawa, Wach's student at the University of Chicago, gives an excellent introduction to Wach and his life in Joachim Wach's book, *The Comparative Study of Religion* (New York: Columbia University Press, 1958), xiii–xlviii.

2. What is the Chicago School of the study of religion? Wach stressed that the study of religion at Chicago included three facets: the theoretical (study of belief systems), the practical (the way religions are practiced), and the institutional (how religious values shape the religion's institutions). After Wach, many significant religious studies scholars followed this school of thought, including Mircea Eliade, Joseph Kitagawa, Jonathan Smith, Wendy Doniger, Frank Reynolds, Charles Long, and Lawrence Sullivan.

of Religion.[3] In these books and in scores of essays, he unfailingly has important things to say about the way in which the student approaches such questions as the role of objectivity and subjectivity in the study of religion, the capacity of believers and nonbelievers to fully understand the religions they are studying, and the attitude required for a religion student to succeed at his or her scholarship.

In an effort to capture some of this important information, I will frame it with the central question of this book, *Why study religion?*, in conjunction with the specific question of this chapter, *How should a student choose whether to study religion?* That is, what aptitudes and skills are the best predictors of success and satisfaction when it comes to studying the religions of the world?

Objectivity and Empathy

Much of what Wach has to say must be put in the context of his life as a German survivor of Nazi persecution. Most of his family died in Nazi concentration camps. He felt a great deal of what might be called "survivor's guilt" at being able to build a new life in the United States; many of his family members did not escape the holocaust. Because religion played a consequential role in the evil designs of Nazi ideology, it would have been surprising if Wach had not dealt at length with the role of bias, prejudice, and persecution in the study of religion.

He doesn't disappoint. In a very real sense, Wach's personal situation in the 1940s anticipates the interreligious angst that faces the world today. Anti-Semitism remains with us still, growing more virulent in patches across Europe and the United States. But anti-Semitism has been joined by religious prejudices and terrorisms affecting all the religious groups of the world. Anti-Christianism grows at home and abroad. Anti-Islamism, as a response to terrorism carried out in the name of Islam, continues to increase. Religious wars around

3. Wach's major works are *Religionwissenschaft* (Leipzig: Hinrichs, 1924); *Introduction to the History of Religions* (New York: Macmillan, 1988); *Sociology of Religion* (Chicago: University of Chicago Press, 1944); and *Types of Religious Experience: Christian and Non-Christian* (Chicago: University of Chicago Press, 1951).

the world affect Hindus, Buddhists, Confucians, and Sikhs, all of whom experience deadly persecutions in many places.[4] One can even make a case for the growth of antireligionism in general, as antireligious humanists of one sort or another confront religions with their shadow sides.

In the midst of his own crisis, Wach makes clear that the history of religion is not to be seen as parallel with the "love truth, hate untruth" paradigm of many philosophical and ethical systems. Wach maintains that one needs to be able to champion religion in general and one's own faith in particular, without denigrating other religions. According to Wach, this is the great value of the scientific study of religion:

> It is true that to love truth you must hate untruth, but it is not true that in order to exalt your own faith you must hate and denigrate those of another faith. A comparative study of religions such as the new era made possible enables us to have a fuller vision of what religious experience can mean, what forms its expression may take, and what it might do for man. It could be argued that this would mean the subjection of one's religious faith to a judgment pronounced in the name of some generalized notions. But does a ruby or an emerald sparkle less if called a jewel?[5]

If scholarly expertise is assumed here, what else is required of the student of religion to be able to demonstrate this kind of attitude toward religions that are not one's own? In a few places, Wach proposes something he calls "empathy." For Wach, "religion is something toward which neutrality is impossible."[6] But that still leaves the field open to all kinds of emotions and passions regarding religion. Wach is calling for something somewhere between indifference and zealousness, whether born of hostility or deep faith: "If it is the task of theology to investigate, buttress, and teach the faith of a religious community to which it is committed, as well as to kindle zeal and

4. Consider the excellent work on the origin and nature of religious violence done by Mark Juergensmeyer, especially his Grawmeyer award-winning *Terror in the Mind of God: The Global Rise of Religious Violence* (Berkeley: University of California Press, 1999).

5. Wach, *Comparative Study of Religion*, 9.

6. Ibid.

fervor for the defense and spread of this faith, it is the responsibility of a comparative study to guide and purify it."[7]

What happens in the world when this kind of empathetic attitude is displayed toward others' religions, not only by religion scholars but by anyone who comes in contact with a religious belief or a religious adherent with whom he or she disagrees? Put simply, the world's peace quotient among religions increases. When we realize that we have better ways to approach other religions than the ones most often presented in our histories—war, conflict, persecution, and hatred of the other—we find ourselves in a position to better our world by bettering ourselves, especially in the way we view other religions.

This attitude of generosity toward other religions is not necessarily acceptance but rather a spirit of what Wach calls "an engagement of feeling, interest, *metexis*, or participation."[8] As such, the whole world benefits. Antipathies among religions lessen. Everyone benefits from a more guilt-free practice of their own religion, knowing that others are similarly inspired. Wach believed that the study of religion could bring to the world's religions the same irenic spirit that by all accounts was a feature of Wach's own personality.

As the world has become increasingly complex and as cultures and people groups have truly become multicultural, multiethnic, and multiracial (as a result of emigrations, diasporas, and worldwide connectivity through social media), the role of religion ("good" religion at least) has slowly shifted. In premodern times religion functioned chiefly as an identity marker; in modern cultures it has been a meaning-maker. And while it still retains remnants of those functions today, religion is increasingly becoming one of our sole means of integrating otherwise disparate human groupings. Religion may be our last best hope at establishing real community.[9]

In the fifty-plus years since Wach's death, religious studies as a discipline has continued to grow. Each November, nearly ten thousand

7. Ibid.
8. Ibid., 12.
9. See the conclusion to this book for further discussion regarding this suggestion that religion's role in human societies has changed over the years from identity marker to meaning maker to community builder.

professors of religion gather at the annual meeting of the American Academy of Religion to discuss the results of their latest research among their peers. I have attended these meetings annually for the past forty-four years, the last thirty-four of which have included the meetings of the Society for Buddhist Christian Studies. While the scholarship presented at the meetings has taught me a great deal, I have also been honored to build a score of lasting friendships with scholars from across the country and around the world.

Scholarship

An argument can be made that no academic discipline has better anticipated the postmodern turn, especially in terms of method, than religious studies. Back in the days of World War II, Wach would not have understood the previous sentence, particularly the phrase *postmodern turn*. But many of his descriptions concerning what it takes to be a good student of religion sound hauntingly familiar and might even lend evidence to an audacious claim: religious studies students and researchers are on the cutting edge of scholarship when it comes to a clear understanding of what human beings can and cannot know. Let me cite just two examples as evidence of this claim.

Religious Studies Is Syntonic

Syntonic is Wach's term for the way in which a good religious studies scholar must strike a mediating position somewhere between apologetics and laissez-faire indifference.[10] Apologetics can be left to the theologians, and indifference serves no scholar well. Wach argues that in order to understand any phenomenon, one must have some kind of emotive engagement with it, and the best emotion to bring to the table of religious studies scholarship is empathy. Empathy is not agreement, nor is it a shortchanging of critical thinking. It is simply

10. In *Comparative Study of Religions*, Wach presents this idea in some detail. Rudolf Otto, in his book *The Idea of the Holy*, trans. John W. Harvey (1917; repr., New York: Oxford University Press, 1958), calls this the *sensus numinis*—i.e., an ability to experience *numinous* feelings. Just as the description of color in painting or pitch in music requires certain kinds of perceptual abilities, so does the study of religion.

an attitude that enables the researcher to be open to discovery in a field that is chock-full of the unexpected and the exotic.

Syntonic, as Wach uses the term, means more than that. It also means that the religious studies scholar must have an affinity with the religion and the culture in which the religion thrives. Max Weber calls this an "elective affinity."[11] Weber isn't talking about the relationship between student and religion but between religion and culture. Wach changes the terms of the affinity slightly and refers it to the insight a scholar gets when he or she approaches a religion and its culture with empathy. Taken together, this approach is syntonic.

Religious Studies Is Interdisciplinary

It is often said that religious studies is a field rather than a discipline because it encompasses so many different research methodologies—history, phenomenology, psychology, linguistics, sociology, anthropology, philosophy, and others. In a very real sense, religious studies swims against the stream of increasing academic specialization by welcoming so many different ways of studying its subject matter. That is not to say that within the field of religious studies there are not academic turf battles taking place. It *is* to say that the way in which religious studies is constructed allows it a certain potential to achieve some of the benefits of real interdisciplinarity, a potential that many other disciplines can only dream of.

Wach goes to some pains to emphasize that religious studies includes not only one's intellectual capacities but one's emotive and volitional capacities as well. In a couple of different places he outlines what it takes to be a religious studies scholar, including the following three categories.[12]

11. Weber's most famous book, *The Protestant Ethic and the Spirit of Capitalism* (New York: Penguin Books, 2002), is the best example of what he elsewhere terms "elective affinity." The "affinity is between the growing economic base of capitalism developing in early Europe and the ethics of protestant Christianity" (8). Because capitalism and Protestant ethics were compatible, both grew as a result of contact with each other.

12. The role of emotions in epistemology is hotly debated. Some argue that in order to fully exercise our critical thinking capacities, emotions must be curtailed. Others recognize the affects as integral parts of critical thinking. I am of the latter

INTELLECTUAL SKILLS

Data. In an age where scholarly research discussions revolve mostly around method and process, there continues to be no substitute for basic data. If one wants to study religion, the basics—that is, the history, beliefs, and practices of the religion—are the baseline from which everything else proceeds.

Language. There is no substitute for knowing the languages— ancient and modern, sacred and secular—in which a religion was formed, written about, and practiced. Hindu scholars must learn Sanskrit and Hindi. Buddhist scholars must know Pali, Sanskrit, and then Tibetan, Mandarin, Japanese, or Korean. Muslim scholars cannot do without Arabic. And all religion scholars must know at least German and French, the European languages of scholarly religious studies.

EMOTIONAL PROCLIVITIES

Empathy. A capacity and willingness to be sympathetic to the religion and the religious is essential.

Syntonic. In addition to empathy, some form of resonance must be kindled by exposure to the religion of study. This resonance may be the result of comparisons with one's own religious tradition or culture.

VOLITIONAL ACTIONS

Constructive Goals. The goals of the religious studies scholar need to be positive, combining a willingness to admire positive features of the religion under study and a desire to see one's scholarly product produce good fruit.

Experience. The religious studies scholar is often called on to participate in the practices of the religion under study. When devoted to scholarly ends, this is often called "participant observation."[13] One's own religious practice often plays a role here, raising some interesting questions about how one's scholarly study relates to one's religious

---

camp and follow the thinking done at the Foundation for Critical Thinking, which is headquartered at Berkeley, California.

13. "Participant observation" is a research technique used especially by cultural anthropologists. Put most simply, it means participating in a culture's ongoing activities while recording observations made as a result of this "insider" view. Participant observation is used almost exclusively in qualitative studies, not quantitative ones.

beliefs. How does one combine the two, knowing that pure objectivity is impossible and pure subjectivity is unreliable?

Religiosity

Is there a religious approach to the study of religion? That is, can someone belong to a religious tradition, believe in it fully, yet still be a religious study scholar?

These may seem like odd questions to most Western scholars of religion. Many if not most of them would answer something like this: the scholarly study of religion had its genesis and continues its existence precisely to create an objective alternative to the so-called Christian (or religious) approach to the study of religion. That is, most scholars of religion see themselves engaged in an enterprise that either brackets theological commitments of any sort or eschews them altogether.[14]

I would like to challenge that view. A number of years ago I remember having a conversation with a scholar of religion about this very topic. At one point in our conversation he said, "What really scares me about evangelical Christians is that they bring a theology to the study of religion." I responded, "What really scares me are scholars who study religion and think that they don't bring a 'theology' to their study of religion."

Everyone brings ultimate value commitments of one sort or another to this scholarly endeavor. Some are explicit and some are implicit. While some scholars are conscious of their commitments, others don't realize what their commitments are, or they don't recognize the impact their commitments make. I also believe strongly in a corollary to the position that we all have ultimate commitments: since we all have regulating commitments of one sort or another (e.g., universals that we expect everyone participating in our scholarly field to

14. This has always seemed (to me) to be an inconsistent argument. In graduate school we often heard that in order to really understand a religion you had to belong to it—the "you must be one to understand one" argument—which seemed totally incompatible with the "you can't be religious" argument. That is, the people we should recruit to teach Buddhism courses need to be Buddhist, those who teach Hinduism must be Hindu, etc. Obviously the two arguments, "you can't be religious" and the "you must be one to understand one," don't fit together very well, if at all.

acknowledge), those commitments necessarily need to be brought to consciousness and articulated so that we can more accurately engage and evaluate one another's work, as well as our own.

Let me try to articulate what I see as the religious commitments a scholar brings to his or her work as a student of religion. It helps to break this general question down into three smaller questions:

1. Objectivity: *Can* a scholar have strong religious commitments and still be an objective religious studies scholar, faithful to all the methodological canons of the religious studies guild?

2. Religiosity: *Should* a religious studies scholar have such commitments? That is, what are the pros and cons of acknowledging one's own religious commitments vis-à-vis the work one does as a religious studies scholar?

3. A Christian example: As a specific example of the effects religious commitments might have on scholarly work, how can we articulate one way to define a Christian approach to the scholarly study of religion? I use the Christian example because I am a Christian and most familiar with Christian theology, but each religious tradition can make his or her own argument here, from the perspective of his or her own tradition.

Objectivity

Can scholars of religion maintain firm religious commitments? This is a difficult way to state a question, for several reasons. It may be that the negative of the question—Can a religious studies scholar *not* be religious?—is a better way to phrase it. Or it could be put this way: since everyone is, if you can't, nobody is. Since everyone is religious in one way or another, if a person is prohibited from being religious and a religious studies student at the same time, then nobody can be a religious studies student. It works as a question only at the level of combating a concern that every scholar, religious or not, struggles with: the danger of letting deeply held biases and prejudices skew negatively the results of one's research.[15]

---

15. My statement about why I chose to study religion in the introduction to this book is an example of stating bias in order to allow for it in the evaluation of my

This method of framing the problem recognizes that either religious feelings and commitments are unavoidably prejudiced and biased or they are the very antithesis of bias and prejudice since they require a self-giving to a higher power, which precludes bias in any form. Frankly, religion can probably be either of these options: a seedbed for bias or a bastion of respectful commitment to truth. Thus one person can be religious and still satisfy all the requirements of objectivity necessary for scholarship, while another person's commitment to religion infects their scholarship with a debilitating virus of subjectivity.

The answer to the question, then, is yes—but it depends on the nature of a person's religious commitments.[16] If part of one's religious commitments is to be honest—to respect one's fellow human beings and to pursue truth, however one's religion defines it—then it is possible. It is impossible if one's religion demands a commitment that ignores so-called truth if it in some way diminishes the impact and control of the religion.

Pure objectivity is impossible.
Pure subjectivity is irrational.
Relative objectivity must be the goal.

One of the earliest of the scholars of religion, Max Müller's compatriot at Oxford, James Legge,[17] the great translator of *The Chinese Classics*, made the case for scholarly research in religion by comparing the way Christian biblical scholars should evaluate the Scriptures and the methods used to evaluate and research any other religious book:

---

research and results. If the reader knows that I grew up as a Baptist evangelical Christian, he or she knows what kind of questions I was trained to ask in different situations. Bias is a rather negative way to express the truth that everyone comes at an issue with a point of view. Skilled researchers who are candid about their point of view—both to readers and to themselves—are more open to other people's points of view.

16. C. S. Lewis is famous for having made the observation that he felt more comfortable with a person of another religion who embraced their religious beliefs with the same intensity (or lack thereof) that he did than he did with another Christian whose understanding of the nature of religious commitment was different from his own.

17. See my comments on Legge's religious studies legacy under the section "A Delightful Complexity" in chapter 4 of this book.

The books of the Old and New Testaments have come down to us just as the Greek and Roman, and Chinese classics have done, exposed in the same way to corruption and alteration, to additions and mutilations. The text of them all has to be settled by the same canons of criticism; the meaning of the settled text has to be determined by similar corresponding processes of construction. The fact that we have in the Christian scriptures a revelation does not affect the method of their study.[18]

Religious Commitment

Should a religious studies scholar be religious? "Should" questions are very big questions, and this one is no exception. So let me limit it by examining just one small aspect. Are there any advantages to the religious studies scholar having vibrant faith commitments of his or her own? I believe there are. In part, my belief picks up on Wach's description of synchronicity. Having faith commitments of one's own deepens one's capacity to understand the nature of the faith commitments held by adherents of other religions. Faith gives insight into faith, belief to belief.[19]

There is an obvious danger here. One cannot impose categories of understanding, practice, and belief on other religions. It is almost a cliché in religious studies departments to watch new religious studies students project their own beliefs onto people of other traditions. "Where is the concept of sin in this religion? As Christians we believe in sin. Where is sin in Buddhism?" It takes effort to learn that just because something is an element of one's own religious tradition does not mean that it also exists in other religious traditions. Still, one's own approach to religion, carefully monitored, can make one aware of insights worthy of exploration when studying another religious tradition.

18. Norman Girardot, *The Victorian Translation of China: James Legge's Oriental Pilgrimage* (Berkeley: University of California Press, 2002), 324.

19. In "Faith and Knowledge," an essay in *Understanding and Believing* (Westport, CT: Greenwood, 1968), 137, Wach puts it this way: "Being rooted in a personal faith—a faith which may well blind one to other things but which, in contrast to the opinion of many, need not do so—does not necessarily mean a disadvantage for him who seeks to understand. The demand of a *tabula rasa* has long been recognized as utopian; and even though such objectivity might be desirable, it is actually impossible."

An Example: A Christian Scholarship of Religion?

To further address the question of religiosity, let me begin with what I have found to be a helpful analogy.[20] Jonathan Edwards, perhaps the quintessential American theologian, asked a similar question about the religious affections (my paraphrase): Is there such a thing as distinctively Christian religious affections? His answer: Christian love looks something like non-Christian human love.[21] Christian love does many of the same things as love expressed by non-Christians, yet it is distinctive because the Christian loves others in obedience to God's commands and in imitation of God's love as much as possible. Most important, the Christian is animated by the spirit of Christ, who changes the character of the Christian's affections.

Something similar applies to a Christian engaged in religious studies. Christians do many, if not most, of the same things that non-Christians, even nonreligious, scholars do when they study religion. They are slaves to the facts. They strive for fairness and objectivity in their descriptions of other religions. They do not prematurely judge the observations they make about the beliefs and practices of other religions. In short, they look very much like other members of their scholarly guild.

Yet there *is* such a thing as Christian religious studies, which is distinct from Buddhist religious studies, Hindu religious studies, agnostic religious studies, humanist religious studies, and so on. The distinction lies in three main areas: (1) A Christian brings a distinctive outlook to his or her study, an imagination that supplies a distinct motivation for studying other religions; (2) a Christian, because he or she is a Christian, asks and focuses on certain kinds of questions about other religions that others may or may not ask; and (3) a Christian seeks a distinctive payoff for his or her study of religion, which

20. I used much of what follows in this section in a recently published book, *Handbook of Religion: A Christian Engagement with Traditions, Teachings, and Practices*, ed. Terry Muck, Harold Netland, and Gerald McDermott (Grand Rapids: Baker Academic, 2014), 15–18.

21. Interestingly, John Wesley—after reading Jonathan Edwards's *Religious Affections* (Mineola, NY: Dover, 2013), in which this argument appears—approved of this line of reasoning, one example of the ultimate Wesleyan (Wesley) agreeing with the ultimate Calvinist (Edwards).

CHRISTIAN RELIGIOUS STUDIES

A Christian religious studies looks very similar to the religious studies practiced by other religious studies scholars, and it wholeheartedly embraces the values shared by the religious studies guild:

Accuracy
Fairness
Objectivity
Respect

Yet at three distinct points Christians go above and beyond the tenets required by the guild:

1. The Christian religious studies imagination
2. The Christian framework of questions
3. The Christian goal

From Terry Muck, Harold Netland, and Gerald McDermott, eds., *Handbook of Religion* (Grand Rapids: Baker Academic, 2014), 17.

is to say that a Christian has a distinct goal for the study of religion. Let's treat each of these in turn.

THE CHRISTIAN IMAGINATION[22]

When Christians study the religions, they do so within the following context: Christians believe that God is the ultimate creative power in the universe. God created everything, and God created the world good. By giving human beings dominion over the rest of creation, as well as the distinctive gift of free choice of relationship with God, different ways of approaching God (or not approaching God at all) are not only possible but also have been actualized. The religions, Christians believe, are a result of this diversity of choice. When Christians study religions, their theological assumptions include the following understandings: religions have developed as a result of God's created order; each of the religions is more or less good and bad (good creation flawed by human sin); and people who are members of other religions are created by God, in God's

22. See Paul Harris, *The Work of the Imagination* (London: Blackwell, 2000).

image. The Christian student of religions is open to the possibility that the religions have a spiritual dimension—the religions are not only human creations but in some cases also spiritual phenomena caused by spiritual forces.[23] When we study religions we are studying phenomena that have resulted in large part from the universal God-given human desire to know and relate to God, with both good and bad success.

Working within this motivational context, Christian scholars of religion do many of the same things that non-Christian scholars of religion do, but because of this context they may be doing those things for different reasons. The Christian motivation is to learn more about God's created order and the ways in which different peoples of the world, knowingly or unknowingly, try to realize their true nature by reaching out for a creator whom they know only partially (as a result of general revelation, arising from nature and consciousness) or of whom they are only dimly aware.

CHRISTIAN QUESTIONS

For people who are self-consciously Christian, the comparative exercise—recognizing both similarities and differences—is a normal one. Christians choose the Christian way of reaching out to God for many reasons, but one of those ways is usually because they think the Christian way is the best way to reach out to God—the only way that will bring salvation. From observation, Christians know that in the world of religion there are bad ways to reach out to God (e.g., Satanism). However, they also see the good ways in which people in other religions reach out to what Christians believe is God. Therefore, Christians are comfortable asking questions that are comparative in nature. Like all religion scholars their initial questions seek answers of fact. But observation inevitably leads to evaluation, perhaps first of the psychological and sociological effects of different religious traditions but soon after to moral and theological effects as well. For Christian scholars of religion, these questions need not diminish the objectivity of their study; indeed, a loss of objectivity to unacknowledged partisanship would be just as damaging to the Christian

23. I should say that *some* Christian students acknowledge this. Not all do.

scholar of religion as to the humanist scholar of religion or the Buddhist scholar of religion.

CHRISTIAN GOALS

Finally, the Christian scholar of religion admits that his or her final goal in any of life's endeavors, including the study of religion, is to be a better follower of the creator God and the creator God's Son. When faithfully followed, Christians believe that this goal—rather than a more temporal goal—helps to make Christians better scholars of religion.

In the end, a combination of objectivity and empathy, good scholarly research skills and language acquisition abilities, and a kind of personal religiosity that manages to combine intense personal commitment with respect for others are the best predictors of who will be a good student of religion. While you may already possess these aptitudes and skills, you may also be developing them as you come to understand what is required in your studies.

Why I Study Religion

CHARLES FARHADIAN, WESTMONT COLLEGE

Let me begin with two vignettes that illustrate some reasons why I became interested in studying religion. The first story is about my early childhood. I was raised and baptized in the Armenian Apostolic Church in Oakland, California. When I was about ten years old, my mom had a dramatic conversion experience. She told the family that the Armenian Church was concerned only with culture. It did not preach the gospel, so we needed to find a church that did. We settled on the Swedish Evangelical Covenant Church, where I spent the next few decades. Even as a young boy I thought it strange that we had substituted the Swedes for the Armenians and Swedish meatballs for Armenian shish kabobs. We left our family of

Ohanesians, Bedrosians, and Harotoonians and entered the family of Carlsons, Johnsons, and Larsons.

The second experience took place when I was a senior in high school. On a Sunday evening the church showed a film called *Peace Child*, which portrayed Christian missionary activities and the use of redemptive analogies to communicate the gospel to the Sawi people on the south coast of Irian Jaya, now called West Papua, Indonesia. I was engrossed by the portrayal of Sawi Christianity, particularly the vision that Christianity can "look so different" when it was adapted to a Melanesian culture. The idea that rather than losing their culture, Sawi ritual longings were fulfilled through the Christ event captivated me; their ritual of giving a "peace child" to an enemy clan as a sign and promise of peacemaking was analogous to Christian redemption. Months after viewing that film I had the opportunity to live in that same Sawi village for the summer, a summer that changed my life. The questions and curiosities that emerged for me while in West Papua about the relationship between gospel and culture have fueled my education and intellectual life ever since.

So why study religion? Learning religion moves me in two important directions. First, by studying religion I encounter the other; that is, I have the opportunity to learn about other people, cultures, histories, societies, and philosophies. As such, studying religion has enriched my view of God, human nature, and the natural and supernatural world. Second, studying religion interrogates the familiar; that is, as I study religion I am invited to deepen my appreciation of Christian faith, in large part because I see Christian faith from another's perspective, learn about what is unique and similar about Christianity and other religions, and have the opportunity to be reshaped by what I encounter.

As I have taught various religious traditions I have become more convinced of their grandeur, insights, and wisdom. At the same time, I increasingly recognize that while Christianity shares significant similarities with other religions, there are also unique features of Christian faith and the gospel that compel my life and thinking. That double movement of encounter and interrogation allows me to more fully embrace the insights and religionists of other traditions. While I certainly have much to learn, I also have, in the words of Lesslie Newbigin, the "bold humility" to give expression in word and deed to the Christ event that I believe transforms all of life.

PART 2

WHY NOW?

As a new student of religion, you should know why religious studies is important, not just in a general sense, in all times and in all places, but also in a particular sense—at this time (early twenty-first century) and in this place (both the West and globally). As you can probably tell, I think religious studies has been important since its founding in the late nineteenth century. But I also think it is especially important right now. What is it about the world in which we live that makes the study of religion so crucial, useful, and interesting? That's the rationale the three chapters in part 2 provide.

Chapter 3 looks at the changes in social structure that are sweeping the globe. A new form of radical freedom seems to be accompanying democratic pluralisms and mixing freely with some of the most restrictive totalitarianisms known to humankind. How does this manifest itself in the religious expressions of the world?

Chapter 4 examines the nature of individual religious identity, making special note of the term *religious hybridity*, which refers to the capacity that modern and (especially) postmodern individuals have to "mix and match" their beliefs and practices when it comes to religion. How can one be Christian and Buddhist at the same time? Read this chapter to find out the argument made by people who believe this can done.

Chapter 5 addresses one of the most crucial aspects of modern-day living—the growing presence of religiously motivated conflict around the world—that leads to unprecedented levels of religious terrorism, religious persecution, and religious martyrdom. It is accurate to say with Christian theologian Hans Küng that "there will be no peace among the peoples of the world until there is peace among the religions of the world."[1]

If you are not a first-time student but have taken a few courses in religious studies, you will recognize the subject matter of these three chapters. However, because of your experience you might read chapters 3, 4, and 5 a bit differently from the way a first-time student would read them. For example, you will have already been exposed to sociologists of religion like Robert Bellah who talk about how sociological differentiation translates into religious differentiation; you might ask why this radical differentiation is taking place now. Or you might go beyond the discussion of the way in which complex religious identities make personal religious expression a creative endeavor to ask whether there is a limit to the amount of complexity that is possible before the whole idea of a person's religious identity loses its meaning. Perhaps the discussion of the clash of religions in chapter 5 will lead to questions of whether the study of religions can, or does, actually change the way religions "clash" with one another.

I would like to suggest that chapter 3 can be read with a greater focus on how archaic religious expressions, modern religious expressions, and postmodern religious expressions all have a role to play in the cultures in which we live. That is, how do these expressions combine to produce our default ways of looking at religion today? I will deal with this question in more detail in chapter 7.

Chapter 4 can be read with greater focus concerning the uniqueness of religious hybrid identity. For example, what if one read William James's *Varieties of Religious Experience*—which suggests that there are four main types of religious personalities—in light of the recent

1. Hans Küng used this quote in several of his books and often in his speeches. See Küng, *Islam: Past, Present and Future* (Oxford: Oneworld, 2007), xxiii.

phenomenon of hybridity? One result of such a reading could be the observation that there are no purely sick-souled or healthy-minded religious people (to use his terms), but only combinations of the two.

At the end of chapter 5 the obvious question to address is whether the religious clashes of the future can be tipped in the direction of respectful, peaceful contacts rather than antagonistic, confrontational ones. Although as religious studies scholars we are not tasked with trying to make that happen, who among us would not hope that the fruits of our scholarly researches would not in some way contribute to that kind of interaction?

3

Changing Societies

Radical Differentiation

Religion cannot exist independent of a social structure of some kind. Although religion is often thought of and described in individual, personal terms, a religion is by nature a communal exercise. Religions that stand the test of time are made up of many believers, and those believers must associate with one another. By and large, each major religion is made up of a group of people, a community of believers. And that community, whatever it is called in a particular tradition (Christians call it the church), must relate somehow to the larger society in which it exists. Religions are communal affairs, existing as communities within communities.

This social aspect of religion is a big deal not only internally—that is, in how a religion structures itself—but also in terms of how any particular religion relates to the wider society in which it exists. How does a religion relate to the other religions that may exist within that particular society, to the economic and political structures of that society, and to individuals who do not belong to the religion? How does it relate to friends or to enemies in the wider culture? How does it relate to young people in the culture and to old people? How does this particular religion relate to the various ethnic groups that exist in the culture? Does it draw its membership largely from one ethnic group or from many ethnic groups?

Scholars of religion who deal primarily with religions and the relationship of those religions to their social environment are called "sociologists of religion." Sociology of religion is one of the largest subgroups within the alliance of disciplines that make up the field of religious studies, and it has produced some of the biggest names in the discipline as a whole: Max Weber, Émile Durkheim, Clifford Geertz, and Robert Bellah, just to mention a few. These sociologists of religion deal with questions about who belongs to different religious groups, why they join those groups, how the groups organize themselves, and who leads them.

This chapter focuses on these questions and the scholars of religion who study them—that is, sociologists of religion. In addition, it focuses primarily on this statement: when social structures change, the religions associated with them change. I want to focus on this particular issue because part of the answer to the question of this book, *Why Study Religion?*, is related to the fact that one of the biggest reasons to study religion is to understand the different forms religion takes in the world today. These forms are different in large measure because of the changes that are occurring in social structures across the globe.

In order to structure this discussion of structure, I focus on two concepts that characterize the relationships that religions have with social structures: differentiation and function.

Differentiation

Differentiation is defined by sociologists in the following way:

> The principle feature of modern society is the increased process of system differentiation as a way of dealing with the complexity of its environment. This is accomplished through the creation of subsystems in an effort to allow more variation within the system in order to respond to variation in the environment.[1]

1. George Rizer, *Contemporary Sociological Theory and Its Classical Roots* (New York: McGraw-Hill, 2007), 95–96.

To see how this sociological theory relates to religion, a bit of (recent) sociological history is in order.

In the 1960s, University of Chicago sociologist Talcott Parsons wrote a book (*The Evolution of Societies*) in which he describes a theory of social action that characterizes modern Western societies.[2] He suggests that four systems dominate: political, economic, social, and cultural. He calls such societies "differentiated" because social functions that had been generalized across social groupings in the premodern age became specializations in the modern age. The reason for this specialization, Parsons says, is to expand each sector's ability to adapt to increasingly complex social situations. In Parsons's theory of social action, he suggests that religion became a specialty located within the cultural system. One of Parsons's students, Robert Bellah, focused his work on that dimension of religion, writing the well-known essay "Religious Evolution,"[3] in which he describes in historical detail the increasing complexity and accompanying differentiation that characterizes modern religion. We will take a look at this essay in detail in a moment.[4]

After examining Bellah's essay, I suggest that today we need to go beyond the type of differentiation described by Bellah and Parsons. Religion in the twenty-first century rarely exists in its premodern form as part of an undifferentiated tribal culture in which beliefs and practices seem to be part of a seamless and largely unreflected-upon whole. But religion in the twenty-first century is also moving beyond the compartmentalized, often privatized, differentiated phenomena observed by modern sociologists such as Parsons and sociologists of religion such as Bellah. Religion today is neither undifferentiated nor differentiated, if by differentiated we mean that religion has its own cultural compartment alongside its political compartment, its economic compartment, and its social compartment in the broad social system. Instead, religion today is *radically* differentiated.

2. Talcott Parsons, *The Evolution of Societies* (New York: Prentice Hall, 1977).
3. Robert Bellah, "Religious Evolution," in *Beyond Belief: Essays on Religion in a Post-Traditional World* (New York: Harper & Row, 1970), 20–50.
4. More recently, Bellah used these ideas in his seminal essay to create his magnum opus: Robert Bellah, *Religion in Human Evolution: From the Paleolithic to the Axial Age* (Cambridge, MA: Belknap Press of Harvard University Press, 2011).

RELIGIOUS DIFFERENTIATION

In premodern times, societies tended to be undifferentiated religiously—religion and other social functions tended to blend together. In modern times, societies became increasingly differentiated religiously, with institutions and religious leaders separated and clearly defined over against each other. As we move into postmodernity, societies and cultural systems are becoming radically differentiated. In current cultures, especially in urban areas, one can find manifestations of all three types of religion.

Undifferentiated (Premodern)

Political	Economic
Social	Religion Cultural

Differentiated (Modern)

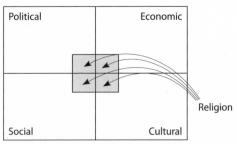

Radically Differentiated (Postmodern)

From Terry Muck, Harold Netland, and Gerald McDermott, eds., *Handbook of Religion* (Grand Rapids: Baker Academic, 2014), 7 (developed with information from Talcott Parsons, *The Evolution of Societies* [Englewood Cliffs, NJ: Prentice Hall, 1997] and Robert N. Bellah, *Beyond Belief* [1970; repr., Berkeley: University of California Press, 1991]).

What we see happening in the years since Parsons did his seminal work is an increasing differentiation within each of his major social spheres—the political, economic, social, and cultural. Most interesting to this study, however, is that the presence of religion, in the form of new religious movements, is evident in all these spheres, not just the cultural. There are political religious expressions (Hindutva, Christian Identity), economic religious expressions (Marxism, Prosperity Gospel), and social religious expressions (the Amish religion, the Moonies) as well as cultural expressions. Religion is everywhere and expresses itself in nearly any societal form one can imagine. We call this radical differentiation.[5] The following illustration looks more closely at the new religious movement phenomenon.

New Religious Movements

The term *new religious movements* (as "new" implies) refers to groups that have grown up in modern societies in the past two hundred years. Wherever there are modern societies, there are new religious movements; wherever there are new religious movements, there are modern societies.

A modern society has a number of features:

- a reliance on rationalistic models of thinking
- a dependence on the scientific method
- leadership based on the authority of office
- a bias toward market economics[6]

In terms of new religious movements, however, one feature of modernity is paramount. To use a sociological term, modern societies are *differentiated*. That is, they have a number of systems that are both dependent on one another and independent of one another—a

5. In "Between Religion and Social Science" in *Beyond Belief*, even Bellah recognizes that we are moving to something beyond modern religion and its complexity: "Differentiation has gone about as far as it can go" (257).

6. Terry Muck, Harold Netland, and Gerald McDermott, eds., *Handbook of Religion: A Christian Engagement with Traditions, Teachings, and Practices* (Grand Rapids: Baker Academic, 2014).

political system, an economic system, a social system, a cultural system, a personality system, and a behavioral system.

New religious movements tend to find their reason for being in one or another of these six systems. The majority of these movements, of course, derive from the cultural system of a traditional or world religion. Transcendental meditation, for example, is rooted in Hinduism but has been transplanted to Western therapeutic culture. The Church of Jesus Christ of Latter-day Saints is a reinterpretation of Christian history, belief, and practice (or as Mormons would probably say, a restoration of true Christianity).

Some new religions come from the social system. Their reason for being is to augment social systems designed to allow people to live together harmoniously. Freemasonry, for example, is sometimes described as a social club; its raison d'être is to encourage community. It uses religious terminology, derived largely from Christianity, to build that community. As a result, Freemasons insist that they are just a social club, though others wonder about their use of religion and religious language.

Other new religions have political emphases. Christianity and religion in the United States, for example, share political symbols—such as a country, a flag, patriotism, and holidays—to encourage a sharper identity between God and country. Christian Identity, on the contrary, is a new religious movement that uses political symbols as a form of resistance to prevailing political patterns.

Several new religious movements seem most at home using economic symbolism. The most outstanding twentieth-century example is Marxism, an ideology based on an economic deprivation metaphysic. Some economic groups, such as the Landmark Forum, exist to elevate participation in market capitalism to a religious level. Some people would say that all religions in modern societies are heavily influenced by market economics—for example, what some Christians call the "prosperity gospel."

Western therapeutic cultures tend to elevate individualism to premier status. This focus on the nature of personality has led to the popularity of religions such as Scientology and the human potential movement, which consider individual physical health to be the Holy Grail of modern living.

Finally, the revival of some ancient indigenous religions such as neopaganism represents an attempt to reclaim an almost biological identification with nature and our genetic core. These old/new religious movements rely on instinct- and intuition-based epistemologies, in addition to the web of all being as a metaphor of existence.

Religion in differentiated modern societies plays a dual role. It provides both meaning and motivation. Traditionally, religion has always provided meaning to human adherents. Parsons considers religion to be perhaps the first adaptive response of human beings to unexplained, seemingly random suffering, such as disease, death, and natural disasters. Throughout human history and across human religious symbol systems, one can see religion enabling us to better cope with and control our environment.

In the modern era, however, religion provides an additional coping function, which can be encapsulated in the word *integration*. Although the differentiation of modern societies provides enormous adaptive capacity, it also creates an unintended consequence. Fragmentation of the social system leads to the loss of an integrating center, which in turn leads to a potential loss of meaning and results in growing existential anxiety.

In such a social system, religious symbol systems succeed or fail based on the extent to which they can integrate diffuse, competing meanings and thus relieve anxiety. For example, the economic system conveys that meaning comes from making money; the political system indicates that it comes from power acquisition; the social system posits relationships and institutions as the locus of meaning; and the cultural and personality systems maintain that it comes from symbols and personal identity formation.

Religion helps adherents to cope with the confusion created by multiple meanings. Many of the new religious movements use one or another of these social systems as a centering place for integrating multiple meanings. Freemasonry, for instance, addresses existential loneliness by creating a social club, using religious symbolism as a way to further stress the club's importance.

In the process of interpreting meanings, new religious movements also provide motivation for social actors and their acting.[7] Why should

---

7. "Social action" is a term that sociologists usually define as: "Individual or group behavior that involves interaction with other individuals or groups especially organized action toward social reform."

I go against my own economic or political interest to create better social conditions? Because my religious myth describes for me the value of such an action and provides me with the motivation to act on it.

The ways that new religious movements create integrated meanings and motivations vary along two other axes. In addition to choosing one of the six social locations as primary (political, social, economic, cultural, personality, or behavioral), new religious movements can either embrace or resist current religious forms in these spheres (with the choice to reform, revitalize, or reject them). What's more, they can either embrace or resist the temptation to try to organize the social spheres themselves.[8]

Consider the two new religious movements I mentioned that represent the economic system: Marxism and the Landmark Forum. Karl Marx saw his teaching as resisting and revolutionizing the current bourgeoisie dominance of economic production. "Workers of the world unite!" he said, advocating an overthrow of current political systems. The Landmark Forum, on the other hand, fully embraces the prevailing economic form of market capitalism, protecting it and encouraging adherents to take full advantage of it.

Consider also the cultural system, which is the usual location of the traditional historic religions, including Christianity. As a new religious movement, the Church of Jesus Christ of Latter-day Saints (Mormons) embraces Christianity but seeks to restore it to (what the Mormons believe to be) its original form and intent. Satanism, on the contrary, exists primarily to counter every Christian value and advocates the elevation of what could accurately be described as anti-Christianity.

New religious movements embody the trend of seeing the "relationship to the ultimate as no longer the monopoly of the historic religions."[9] Religious symbolism emerges from everywhere in the modern social system—political speeches, television advertisements, and pop culture songs and imagery. Many of the religions of this system are the organizations and institutions that have emerged from this movement that is moving us all toward an embrace of domesticated transcendence.

8. Muck, Netland, and McDermott, *Handbook of Religion*, 457–60.
9. Bellah, "Religious Evolution," in *Beyond Belief*, 41.

Robert Bellah's Religious Evolution

In chapter 1, I took pains to make the point that evolution, in its scientific and ideological forms at least, proves to be a dead-end theory for religious studies scholars. Both scientific and ideological evolution posit (1) one consistent developmental pattern, (2) consistent progress from one stage to another, and (3) a more-recent-is-better mentality. When scholars look at the history of religion, however, they find none of those things. There is no consistent developmental pattern. As religions "developed" there was almost as much regress as progress. As a matter of fact, the oldest religions—the primitive and archaic forms—were represented by people who, as available evidence indicates, were/are every bit as religious as the modern and postmodern practitioners. As sociologist of religion Bellah puts it, "I do not assume that evolution is inevitable, irreversible, or must follow any single particular course."[10] But he still makes the argument that an evolutionary pattern can be detected within the sociological dimensions of religion; when it comes to the differentiation of religious institutional forms, a consistent pattern of development emerges.

Bellah defines religion simply as "a set of symbolic forms and acts that relate man to the ultimate conditions of his existence" and evolution as "the process whereby more complex forms develop from less complex forms and that the properties and possibilities of more complex forms differ from those of less complex forms."[11] In both definitions, the word *forms* occupies a central place. Furthermore, those forms change. Bellah is not arguing that the essences or realities to which religious symbol systems point necessarily change or evolve or even that the people using those forms to connect with the essences or realities change. He is arguing that the forms that connect realities and humanities change so that the connections between the two can be maintained or even improved by becoming more complex.

Bellah also argues that the way in which the forms change over time can be separated into five stages of religious complexity: primitive, archaic, historic, early modern, and modern. According to Bellah, the stages move from simple forms to complex forms or from complex

10. Ibid., 24.
11. Ibid., 26.

forms to more simple ones. Furthermore, the stages are not mutually exclusive of one another. Primitive forms can continue to exist even when the dominant forms are modern, and so forth. In other words, Bellah uses the stages not as a procrustean bed (his metaphor) into which all religion must be historically shoehorned but as a way to talk about the different forms symbolic human religion takes.

Let's look at each of the stages as Bellah describes them. *Primitive religion* uses its religious symbols to describe a timeless, mythical world.[12] That world and its denizens are not addressed or propitiated or beseeched. Rather, the mythical world is participated in and identified with. Primitive religious men and women attempt to imitate the mythical world in the world in which they now live; for example, they might name mountains and rivers in this world after mountains and rivers in the timeless. Since this imitation includes everything, religious structures and institutions are not separate from other structures. It is a world that includes everywhere and everywhen. In terms of social implications, this kind of religious symbol system offers a very high degree of social solidarity. Everyone is included in everything. This type of primitive religion is especially characteristic of Australian tribal religions.

In *archaic religion*, mythical beings begin to evolve into divine beings worthy of worship and propitiation.[13] In addition to religious actions being heavily ritualized, they are also cultic; one does not interact with beings in the mythical world in a general way but rather as beings worthy of adoration and control. As with primitive religion, the religious organization of archaic religion is largely monolithic, but some differentiation occurs with a multiplication of cults or ways of addressing and appeasing the divine. A priestly caste, for example, develops and performs the needed rituals. As far as social action implications are concerned, Bellah says that "traditional social structures and social practices are considered to be grounded in the divinely instituted cosmic order, and there is little tension between religious demand and social conformity."[14] Archaic religion is especially characteristic of African and Polynesian

12. Ibid., 25–28.
13. Ibid., 29–32.
14. Ibid., 31.

religions, as well as the earliest religions of the Middle East, India, and China.

Historic religion is transcendent in the sense that a separate realm of existence is postulated, over against the everyday world in which we live.[15] Gone is cosmological monism, the identification of this world with the mythic world, and here to stay is a cosmological dualism, a division between an ideal world to be embraced and a mundane world to be rejected. Religious action in such a world is aimed at salvation from the mundane world and/or enlightenment regarding one's delusional views of it. This rejection and education requires a clearer conception of the self than exists at the primitive and archaic levels. An individual religious actor is required to do the rejecting and enlightening. In terms of social organization, the differentiation of the transcendent world from the mundane world requires a differentiation of the religious and the political institutions; with historic religions we see the beginnings of a movement toward the differentiation that Parsons describes for modern times. Rebellion from or reform and rejection of the mundane world becomes religiously possible, with the transcendent providing the rationale for each.

As for *early modern religion*, it is almost as if Bellah created the category solely to explain the Protestant Reformation.[16] Early modern religion continues many of the features of historic religion—transcendent dualism, world rejection, and individualism. Much less emphasis is placed on asceticisms (such as monasticism), and in terms of social organization far fewer hierarchical structures are evident. Early modern religion emphasizes a total religious lifestyle. While social institutions continue to differentiate, they are meant to be open to the religious actor influencing them for the good; in turn, the religious actor is to be positively influenced by the social institution.

Today, we are living in the *modern religion* era. "The modern [religious] situation represents a stage of religious development in many ways profoundly different from that of historic religion. The central feature of the change is the collapse of the dualism that was so crucial to all the historic religions."[17] Bellah goes on to say that

15. Ibid., 32–35.
16. Ibid., 36–39.
17. Ibid., 39–42.

monism and dualism as cosmological religious symbolic forms have been replaced by "an infinitely multiplex" set of forms.[18] We live in an age of runaway religious individualism, an insight that Bellah develops much further in the classic work, *Habits of the Heart*.[19] The main social implication of this de facto religious pluralism is that each of us are faced with unparalleled religious freedom—relatively unchecked by hierarchies, dogmas, and even cultural forces. Whether this freedom is a blessing or a curse is the question Bellah leaves for new researchers to engage.

Functions of Religion

Concurrent with the evolutionary pattern of religious sociology that Bellah outlines in his essay is an observable change in the function religion has played at these various stages. It stands to reason that adherents would come to rely on religion for different things as social and religious differentiation proceeded apace. As the sociologists of religion say, religion at its core is an adaptive human endeavor, that is, a way of living and being that helps people cope with a nervous nature and an unreliable mix of cultures. It may be, as some of the sociologists say, that religion is the primary and most important adaptive behavior human beings have. As societies and their cultures have changed, the nature of our adaptive needs has changed. Three main functions of religion can be observed in the historical journey through which Bellah has just ushered us.

Identity

Seeing religion function as an identity marker fulfills the need of primitive and tribal peoples to answer the question *Who am I?*[20] By answering this question all the other questions are answered by virtue of the well-defined nature of the tribe. To be identified as

18. Ibid., 41.
19. Robert Bellah, Richard Madsen, William M. Sullivan, Ann Swidler, and Stephen M. Tipton, *Habits of the Heart: Individualism and Commitment in American Life* (Berkeley: University of California Press, 1985).
20. Manuel Castells, *The Power of Identity* (Oxford: Blackwell, 1997), 6–12.

"Apache," for example, means others know what you do for a living, where you live, the nature of family life, and your relationship to the cosmos—that is, the nature of your religion. For most of us, religion provides some level of identity, but it is always a qualified identity, a hyphenated identity with disparate elements other than religion.

Meaning

Seeing religion function as a meaning-maker fulfills the need of modern people to find meaning in a highly differentiated world in which plural meaning-making systems are readily available and choices among them must be made. The question meaning-making answers is *What am I here for?* In a real sense this is what Geertz is suggesting when he defines religion as "(1) a system of symbols which acts to (2) establish powerful, pervasive, and long-lasting moods and motivations in men by (3) formulating conceptions of a general order of existence and (4) clothing these conceptions with such an aura of factuality that (5) the moods and motivations seem uniquely realistic."[21] Religion provides a way to choose meaning in life—and provides it in a way that no other element of our social system can.

Relationality

Seeing religion function as a relationship-builder fulfills the need of postmodern people to combat the radically impersonal nature of postmodern living, that is, the lack of community and the off-the-charts nature of independence with which we are forced to cope. In such a culture, the question *Whose am I?* becomes the key to solving the problems of everyday living. As Dorothee Soelle says in her book, *The Mystery of Death*, "Religion's chief end is not to the individual, but to the ability to relate."[22] To some extent religion may still help identify us and give our life meaning, but its chief social function is to help build solidarity among people in societies that are becoming complex to the extent that they are ready to fly apart.

21. Clifford Geertz, "Religion as a Cultural System," in *The Interpretation of Cultures* (New York: Fontana, 1974), 90.
22. Dorothee Soelle, *The Mystery of Death* (Minneapolis: Fortress, 1984), 33.

Thus we see religion move from a simple case of arithmetic, the one-to-one relationship between each of us and our tribes, to a symbol system (not unlike algebra) in which our religious rituals help connect us to the transcendent, to a kind of calculus of relationships, always fluid, always changing in order to keep up with a tremendously accelerated process of social change.

In a very real way, the changes in the function of a religion can be related to the increased complexity of not just modern religion but modern societies and cultures in general. That is, it can be traced to increased differentiation. As societies become more complex, a single identity marker such as religion cannot clearly sum up who a person is. For example, I may identify myself as an American who does not conclusively identify my religion. Even if the percentages would seem to indicate that I, as an American, am most likely a Christian, those percentages would not tell anyone what kind of a Christian I am. Radical religious differentiation is a long way from the function of religion as an identity marker for people who belong to tribal groupings where the religion of tribal members is clear and nonnegotiable. And it is somewhat removed from the modern need for something in our lives that gives meaning.

As we have moved from simple correspondences to symbols to relationships as the essence of religious functionality, we are seeing religion enter a new phase in human flourishing. Religion has always been important in the processes of human community building. It serves as a societal boundary marker and existential touchstone for groups of people in need of both. But what is religion becoming in the twenty-first century?

Where Radical Differentiation Is Taking Us

Many have noted that because of globalization, immigration, and political change we are in an era of unprecedented change. That change is affecting almost every aspect of our society, but let's focus for a moment on how it affects the way religious institutions in particular are changing.

That they are changing seems incontrovertible. What they are changing *to* is less evident. I think it is almost impossible to identify with any confidence, let alone certainty, the new forms of religious institutions in the future. I agree with Hugh Heclo; there will indeed be institutions in our future, but what will they be like?[23] It is very difficult to say.

But difficult does not mean we shouldn't try. Even though I could end this chapter by saying that radical differentiation will proceed apace and for that reason alone we should continue to study religion with all our might, I have decided to go further and do a bit of prognosticating about the future of religious institutions. While I am going to express what I think they might become, underneath that circumlocution the careful reader will see that I am stating what I hope does come to pass.

We might see the following three kinds of religious institutions survive:

Religious institutions that emphasize action as much as (if not more than) theorizing (at least as long as their actions address real societal needs). This does not mean that theorizing (read *theologizing*) will disappear; it just means that it will become a means to an end rather than the end itself. As long as theology is seen as an explanation about, an understanding of, and a justification for an institution's actions, it will be as important as it has ever been. But religious institutions whose rationale has been the preservation of a group's theological heritage will continue to wither, as we have observed for some time with Protestant denominations.

Examples? In addition to denominations, consider theological schools. The schools that exist to perpetuate a tightly proscribed theological "school" will find less and less student support, while those that emphasize training for "mission" (most broadly defined) will continue to attract students. Ecumenical agencies that exist for the abstractly understood notion of church unity will continue to struggle, while those that have a concrete mission will prosper. Interfaith agencies organized simply to talk will not last nearly as long as those agencies that have organized themselves to do.

23. Hugh Heclo, *On Thinking Institutionally* (New York: Oxford University Press, 2011).

Religious institutions that can communicate compassion as much as (if not more than) competition. Am I alone in thinking that three movements crucial to human flourishing—interreligious dialogue, interracial reconciliation, and intereconomic parity—are stuck? Not only that, but they are floundering in the face of religious bias, fear of diversity, and greed. Compassion, if we can muster enough of it, can move all three movements forward. Like theology, compassion is not an end in itself but a means to an end. It is the means used to build the kingdom of God, or whatever a religious tradition calls its ideal state.

Examples? Mission organizations that describe their actions using a business model are doomed. Competition among the religions leads to violence. As Joachim Wach says, when it comes to religion we must abandon the "love truth, hate untruth" paradigm and replace it with the universal paradigm of love and respect for all God's creation.[24] Churches, mosques, and temples that teach separation, suspicion, and suppression of the religious other will not prosper. Churches, mosques, and temples that teach respect, reconciliation, and cooperation will become the leaders in each religion's institutional configuration.

Religious institutions willing to serve any and all existing sectors of their society as much as (if not more than) those that attempt to create sectors of need for their religious product. Call this the response mode, as opposed to the marketing mode. In a way, this observation is consistent with what is already happening. Radical differentiation makes it mandatory that religion and religions, at least the ones that are successful, have the capacity to adapt and influence all sectors of society. This observation is also consistent with what religions have claimed primarily to be—service organizations that help adherents cope and adapt to changing social conditions.

Examples? As a Christian theological educator, I have had the opportunity for the past thirty years to observe young men and women training for Christian ministry. In particular, I have noted the ways in

---

24. Joachim Wach, *The Comparative Study of Religion* (New York: Columbia University Press, 1958), 9.

which they tend to define "ministry."[25] When I first began teaching, ministry referred primarily to serving in an institutional church, like the ones on every other street corner in small-town America. As the years have passed, however, I have seen the definition of ministry broaden far beyond those boundaries. Almost anything done in service to human flourishing can be and is called "ministry" by those involved in it.

What is the best way to summarize how the dramatic changes we see in societal and religious structures and institutions are affecting the ways we study religion? Perhaps such a summary is not possible. Certainly my three prognostications can be debated and improved on. What can be said, with some assurance, is that both society and the church are changing and will continue to change. And that makes the study of religion even more important.

Why I Study Religion

YAAKOV ARIEL, UNIVERSITY OF NORTH CAROLINA

For an Israeli of my generation, choosing religious studies as a scholarly pursuit was unusual. During my high school years, involved as I was in a socialist youth movement and military service, I certainly did not think to pursue religious studies. Matters changed somewhat after I was injured in the Yom Kippur War in 1973. I became convinced of the existence of the *mysterium tremendum* and the guiding spirit of God in the universe. But I did not follow the course of "return to tradition" or "being born again." I visited synagogues and churches, watching, listening, praying, yet exercising some skepticism, and guarding my intellectual and spiritual autonomy. I remained an observer.

25. One of the biggest changes I noticed among my students in theological schools was a dramatic expansion of what they meant when they said they were "going into ministry." In the 1970s this declaration almost always meant taking a local church pastorate, but in the early years of the twenty-first century it came to mean almost anything defined by the student as ministry.

I spent long months as a prisoner of war in the notorious El-Maze prison near Damascus. During that time, my parents registered me as a student of economics at the Hebrew University. I began my studies a few months after returning from captivity but quickly realized that the topic no longer interested me. I shifted my major to history and political science. Still not captivated, I pursued graduate studies in medieval history. This marked the beginning of my engagement with the study of religion. I gravitated toward medieval Christianity, the papacy, the crusades, and religious orders. Although I did not consider studying Judaism specifically, I became convinced that Jewish cultures as I knew them had been strongly influenced by the larger and predominant Christian societies in which Jews lived. Thus I needed a broader perspective on Christianity.

When I finally turned to the department of religious studies, I studied with David Flusser, a scholar of the Dead Sea Scrolls and the New Testament. Flusser became my mentor— a model of a truly independent-minded scholar, rejecting academic fad and fashion. With Flusser's encouragement, I decided to apply to doctoral programs in religious studies across America.

Studying at the University of Chicago was the most rewarding and fulfilling time in my life. Those were years of cultural and mental expansion, and my wife and I thoroughly enjoyed the social and intellectual atmosphere of the place. The University of Chicago had made a reputation for itself as an academic boot camp, and nothing could have suited me better. I admired the broad spectrum of fields, topics, and methods that the program presented. I learned such subjects as Theravada Buddhism with Frank Reynolds and philosophy of religion with Langdon Gilkey. I pursued my interest in medieval Christianity and took a number of courses on Christian thought and mysticism with Bernard McGinn, a towering figure in his field. However, I moved more and more toward studying religion in America. Guided by the amazing scholar and teacher Martin Marty, my doctoral dissertation concentrated on examining the attitudes of American fundamentalists toward Jews and Zionism.

Inadvertently, my studies of Christianity redirected me toward Judaism. For example, when I encountered Christian-Jewish cooperation over Zionism, I discovered that Reform rabbis were among the early leaders and supporters of the movement. Somewhat unexpectedly, I became a scholar of borderline movements in contemporary Judaism and Christianity, such as Christian Zionists, Hasidic hippies, Jewish believers in Jesus, and Jewish returnees to tradition.

Religion studies, as I have discovered throughout my studies, involves much more than extensive learning, careful scholarship, and insightful analyses. It demands respect for the faiths of multiple groups, as well as their recorded and oral scriptures and traditions, communal practices, and cultural heritages. It requires tolerance, patience, and a willingness to listen, read, and constantly learn from others. While this process has been long, it holds great rewards: endless discoveries, personal enrichment, greater openness of mind, and acceptance of the "other."

4

Complex Individuals

Hybrid Personalities

The complexification of human identity, both of oneself and of others, is yet another reason for the importance of studying religion. If the answer to the question *Who am I?* is not so easily answered, and if that answer is further complicated by the answer to the question *Who are you?*, then it follows that the reasons for studying religion are also complex. If nothing else, religion is an affair of personal faith in the transcendent, however it is defined. Therefore, if the "person" in question is nebulous, then the study of what he or she believes becomes something of a social scientific art.[1]

A great deal has been written on the complexity of modern identity, and much of it is centered around the term *hybrid identity*, a concept of personhood first put forward in *The Location of Culture* by Homi Bhabha.[2] Bhabha's basic argument is that our identities are not simple and fixed (essential) but fluid and developing (culturally

1. However, I do not go so far as Wilfred Cantwell Smith on this score. In his *Meaning and End of Religion* (New York: Macmillan, 1962), he asserts that religion is almost entirely a matter of individual faiths.

2. Homi Bhabha, *The Location of Culture* (New York: Routledge, 2004). Another sociologist of religion who has made this point concerning the so-called fluid nature

formed) and that cultural formation in most settings today means formation by multiple cultures. Consider the simplest of examples. Few who live in the United States can claim (or want to claim) that they are simply Americans; they are European Americans (or Irish Americans), African Americans, Asian Americans, Hispanic Americans, and so on.

The reality of this hybridity has implications. For example, social scientists (religion scholars included) need more sophisticated tools to define the subjects of their study. One of the more useful of these research tools is provided by Berkeley sociologist Manual Castells, who parses personal and social identity into three parts: given identity (the unchangeable aspects of our identity, such as place of birth, physical inheritances, etc.), project identity (the parts of identity we develop, such as vocation), and resistance identity (identity elements based on what/who we do *not* want to become). This phenomenological way of looking at identity has real value for scholars attempting to tease out the cultural reasons for and implications of their subjects' behaviors.[3]

In addition to phenomenology, it is important to be able to discern the history of a culture's particular form of hybridity. Social scientists need to know more than just what the Trobriand Islanders *do*. They are immeasurably helped when they can see the cultural forces that created the particular mix of hybrid identity these South Sea denizens make manifest. What indigenous cultural ideas underlay their modern behavior? How have contacts with colonial powers modified those indigenous roots? What postmodern influences, if any, are creating growth points in their lives today? One of the best examples of doing this kind of history is Charles Taylor's *Sources of the Self: The Making of Modern Identity*.[4]

In *Sources*, Taylor details the history of the modern Western person and how he or she views his or her identity. As Taylor describes his own method, he "designates the ensemble of (largely unarticulated)

---

of postmodern human identity is Zygmunt Bauman in *Liquid Times: Living in an Age of Uncertainty* (Malden, MA: Polity Press, 2006).

3. Manual Castells, *The Power of Identity* (Oxford: Blackwell, 1997), 6–12.

4. Charles Taylor, *Sources of the Self: The Making of Modern Identity* (Cambridge, MA: Harvard University Press, 1989), especially 3–21.

understandings of what it is to be a human agent: the senses of inwardness, freedom, individuality, and being embedded in nature which are at home in the modern West."[5] That is, Taylor attempts to dissect and analyze the disparate historical forces that have contributed to the makeup of the modern Western self.

On a much more focused scale, I attempt in this chapter to do what Taylor does in *Sources*. My particular focus is twofold. First, I focus on modern, Western *religious* identity, not identity in general. Religion, despite rumors of its demise, continues to be one of the most important elements of the modern identity. Second, I focus on one specific aspect of religious identity, which involves relating to people of religious traditions other than one's own. As our neighborhoods become conglomerations of world religious adherents, our thoughts and feelings about these new neighbors increase in importance.

Of course, it would be much easier if I could simply say that this book, *Why Study Religion?*, is an argument for studying people by using the scholarly methodologies of social science and history as a way of relating to those who belong to religious traditions that are different from our own. Scholarship is certainly one of several important ways (the other two being mission and interreligious dialogue) of relating to people of other religious traditions. And while it might be easier, and to some extent feasible, to say that this book is just about religious studies, I am not convinced that scholarship alone would lead to the most accurate, nuanced, and rich understanding of why it is we should study religion.

As a scholarly exercise it might work, for heuristic purposes, to separate religious studies from mission and interreligious dialogue. But such an approach would cover up the fact that for most of us all three of these forces—the scholarly, the missional, and the dialogical—contribute to the way we think, feel, and act when it comes to relating to people of other religious traditions. As Taylor so wisely notes in his project, each of the three factors is important and influences the other two. The same is true for this project: the contributions that each of the various elements make to our religious identities in regard to people of other religious traditions may be largely unarticulated. But

5. Ibid., ix.

that makes it all the more important that we bring each of these forces to our consciousness and examine their recent history in our culture as well as their current contributions to our intrareligious psyches.

I believe deeply that not doing this intellectual and psychological excavation of our own souls is what leads to a certain hesitation when it comes to thinking about people of other religious traditions—a hesitation that sometimes manifests itself as confusion, anxiety, and guilt, as well as all too infrequent flashes of respect, fellowship, and engagement. This hesitation impels us, for example, to think that we must choose one approach—mission, dialogue, or scholarship—and deny the other two when we are faced with what seem to be mutually exclusive approaches to the religious other. If we can just see that because of our cultural history all three approaches are deeply ingrained in some form in our interreligious identities, then we can begin to think more clearly about how to proceed. Only then can we focus more clearly and intelligently on the one element that is the special interest of this book: the study of religion.

In this chapter, I look at each of these three understandings, briefly sketch their recent history in Western culture by identifying an important watershed meeting that impelled the growth of each, and then outline the manifestations each is taking in our cultural context today.

The World Parliament of Religions, Chicago, 1893

The World Parliament of Religions was held in Chicago in 1893 as a part of the World Columbian Exposition, a world's fair celebrating the four-hundred-year anniversary of the coming of Christopher Columbus to the North American continent in 1492. The parliament ran from September 11 to September 27 and was held in a building then called the World's Congress Auxiliary Building, which has since become the Art Institute of Chicago. Over four thousand delegates from around the globe, primarily representing the "ten world religions," gave speeches and read papers about the history and demographics of their particular religions. Because the conference focused on the "ten world religions" (Hinduism, Buddhism, Jainism, Confucianism, Taoism, Shintoism, Zoroastrianism, Judaism, Christianity, and Islam were

CHARACTERISTICS OF WORLD RELIGIONS

DEMOGRAPHIC CHARACTERISTICS

Old: The largest world religions (Christianity, Islam, Hinduism, and Buddhism) are thousands of years old. Sociologists would claim that this says something positive about their social utility.

Large: World religions by definition tend to be large. See the study aid, "Religion and Human Rights Exercise."

Cross-cultural: The defining characteristic of a world religion is that it has the capacity to cross cultures and grow in cultural areas in which it did not originate.

ESSENTIAL CHARACTERISTICS

Universal: World religions not only have the capacity to cross cultures but also teach that their doctrines and/or practices have validity for all peoples, everywhere.

World-in-need-of-transformation: Generally world religions operate in a two-tier cosmology, one a spiritual realm and the other a material one. The material realm is to be merely coped with (or denied, or transformed) so that navigation to the more desired spiritual realm is achieved.

Differentiated: World religions tend to have defined sectors in complex, differentiated societies, and operate alongside the other sectors, such as the political, economic, and social.

From Terry Muck, Harold Netland, and Gerald McDermott, eds., *Handbook of Religion* (Grand Rapids: Baker Academic, 2014), 46.

commonly considered the world religions of the day), representatives of indigenous religions, such as African tribal and Native American religions, and (what are now called) new religious movements, such as Mormonism, were largely absent, although Mary Baker Eddy, the founder of Christian Science, was an attendee.

The record of the conference is readily available in two sources. The papers presented at the conference are collected in *The World's Parliament of Religions: An Illustrated and Popular Story*, edited by John Henry Barrows,[6] and *Neely's History of the Parliament of Religions*,

6. John Henry Barrows, ed., *The World's Parliament of Religions: An Illustrated and Popular Story of the World's First Parliament of Religions*, 2 vols. (Chicago: Parliament, 1893).

edited by Walter Houghton.[7] A faithful history and analysis of the meeting, *The World's Parliament of Religions: The East/West Encounter, Chicago, 1893*, was written by Richard Hughes Seager.[8] Numerous other secondary sources can be easily assembled, each of which uses a different lens to focus on various aspects of the parliament.

The two names most often associated with the leadership of the parliament are Charles Carroll Bonney and Barrows. Bonney was in charge of the twenty congresses being held at the World's Fair, and he had a particular interest in the World's Parliament of Religions.[9] He was a Swedenborgian layman; that he belonged to a non-Christian sect perhaps explains his devotion to this particular parliament and why it became the largest—over four thousand people attended the opening-night meeting. Barrows, whom Bonney appointed chairman and chief administrator of the World's Parliament of Religions,[10] was the well-known pastor of the First Presbyterian Church of Chicago. His interest can be gauged in part by the fact that he presided over almost all the sessions held over the seventeen days of the meeting.

The purpose of the World's Parliament of Religions seems as elusive as the motives of the organizers, speakers, and postmeeting commentators. At its most basic, the parliament organizers wanted the meeting to be a celebration of religion in general. A portion of the invitation to the participants reads, "We affectionately invite the representatives of all faiths to aid us in presenting to the world, at the Exposition of 1893, the religious harmonies and unities of humanity, and also in showing forth the moral and spiritual agencies which are at the root of human progress."[11] But the purpose was much more complex than that, for the World's Parliament of Religions

7. Walter Houghton, ed., *Neely's History of the Parliament of Religions* (Chicago: F. T. Neely, 1893).

8. Richard Hughes Seager, *The World's Parliament of Religions: The East/West Encounter, Chicago, 1893* (Bloomington: Indiana University Press, 1995).

9. See Charles Bonney, "The World's Parliament of Religions," *Monist* 5 (April 1895): 321–43.

10. Mary Eleanor Barrows, *John Henry Barrows: A Memoir* (Chicago: Fleming Revell, 1904).

11. Derek Michaud, ed., "World Parliament of Religions 1893," Boston Collaborative Encyclopedia of Western Theology, http://people.bu.edu/wwildman/bce/worldparliamentofreligions1893.htm.

offers evidence of all three elements that characterize our identities as twenty-first-century religious people: scholarship, mission, and dialogue.

Scholarship

The format of the meeting—addresses by participants about their own religions—allowed for a great deal of learning about religions. A perusal of some of the papers shows accounts of religious histories, delineations of belief structures, corrections of misconceptions, and, to some extent, demonstrations of practices (particularly different forms of prayer). Every religion had a chance (typically several chances) to tell its story. Max Müller, the founder of the scientific study of religion, was unable to attend the meeting but went on record as recommending it and expressing the hope that it would further the comparative study of religions in order to "maintain mutual good understanding among the various religious traditions."[12]

Mission

Others seemed to see the World's Parliament of Religions as Christian mission in a new form. A principle commentator on the parliament, Seager, said that Christian triumphalism undergirded the whole endeavor. Although hidden behind explicitly stated goals of tolerance and human brotherhood, the attitude of the organizers and the Christian participants (who represented the majority of participants) displayed an implicit assumption that Christianity was the best religion and the United States was the New Jerusalem. Seager called this the Colombian Myth, claiming that it pervaded the entire World's Fair. He describes it this way: "The Exposition signified the dominant culture of nineteenth-century America as embodying a new Greece or Rome, a repristinated Christianity, and the most highly evolved and enlightened civilization [and religion] in history."[13] For many of the participants and presenters, the mis-

12. Seager, *World's Parliament of Religions*, 126.
13. Ibid., xxxiii.

sional purpose of the conference was not at all implicit. It couldn't be more explicit. One of the Christian speakers, Donald H. Bishop, states this pervasive feeling: "Men need to be saved from false religion; they are in no way of being saved by false religion. Such, at least, is the teaching of Christianity. The attitude, therefore, of Christianity toward religions other than itself is an attitude of universal, absolute, eternal, unappeasable hostility."[14] The mission, by the way, was not limited to Christian participants. Seager considers the parliament to be the beginning of a massive mission undertaken by the Asian religions to the West.[15]

Dialogue

For most commentators, the dominant element of the meeting was relational, though they acknowledged the role of both scholarship and mission at the parliament. More than that, the meeting represented for the first time a gathering of representatives from at least ten of the world religions to talk candidly and frankly about their religion. It was a chance to hear and be heard. Although the phrase *interreligious dialogue* was not yet in vogue at the turn of the twentieth century, dialogicians of today point back to the World's Parliament of Religions as a watershed event in their movement. In Marcus Braybrooke's history of interreligious dialogue institutions, *Inter-Faith Organizations, 1893–1979: An Historical Directory*, he states the greatest value of the meeting as raising the consciousness of Americans concerning religious plurality. Braybrooke begins his history of dialogue with this meeting saying, "No subsequent interfaith gathering has come near to it in its size and complexity."[16] Christian exclusivistic comments and urges aside, Americans were captivated with the presentations of the Asian religionists in particular. The Hindu pundit Vivekananda was easily the most popular speaker of

14. J. H. Barrows, *World's Parliament of Religions*, 1249.

15. Seager, *World's Parliament of Religions*, xvii. Actually, Seager was ahead of his time in recognizing the reciprocal nature of so-called missions among the religions— i.e., seeking converts is not the special province of Christianity and Islam but is also characteristic of Asian religions. Seager calls it the "Asian mission to the West" (xvii).

16. Marcus Braybrooke, *Inter-Faith Organizations, 1893–1979: An Historical Directory* (Lewiston, NY: Edwin Mellen, 1980).

the whole parliament; the meeting started him on a lifelong mission to the West, and he came back to the United States numerous times to found his still thriving Vedanta centers.

The 1893 World's Parliament of Religions in Chicago made a difference in the way we perceive people of other religions. As Seager notes, it "remains an important event in domestic and world history because it is a touchstone by which we can gauge shifts in religious sensibilities."[17] One measure of its enduring value is the popularity of subsequent World Parliament meetings, beginning with the one hundredth anniversary meeting held in Chicago in 1993. Subsequent meetings, drawing anywhere from seven thousand to ten thousand participants, have been held in Cape Town, South Africa; Barcelona, Spain; and Melbourne, Australia. It seems that an enduring part of our human existence, when it comes to people of other religions, is a recognition that respectful conversation must be part of what we do.

International Congress of the History of Religions, Paris, 1900

The 1900 Paris Congress of the History of Religions was held from September 3 to September 8 at the old Sorbonne under the auspices of the *Ecole pratique des Hautes Etudes* of the University of Paris. The organizers compared it to the World Parliament of Religions held seven years earlier in Chicago, both in terms of how it was similar and (more important to them) how it was different. A similarity described by one participant was "its catholicity." That is, "many races, nations, and religions were represented. There were scholars from France and Germany, Italy and Switzerland, Hungary and Russia, Belgium and Holland, Sweden and Norway, England and America, Armenia, India, and Japan. There were Catholics and Protestants, Jews, Brahmins, Buddhists, and Muhammedans."[18] Another similarity was that the congress was part of a much larger

17. Seager, *World's Parliament of Religions*, xx.
18. Nathaniel Schmidt, "The Paris Congress of the History of Religion," *The Biblical World* 16, no. 6 (December 1900): 447.

CHARACTERISTICS
OF INDIGENOUS RELIGION

1. Not cross-cultural: Indigenous religions tend to remain restricted to their culture of origin.
2. Smaller rather than larger: Because of this lack of "missionary" urge, they tend to be smaller.
3. World affirming: Indigenists see the world as an imitation of the gods' world, therefore good and to be affirmed, imitated, and lived with in harmony.
4. Undifferentiated: Religion among indigenous peoples tends not to be separated or compartmentalized from political, economic, and cultural functions.
5. Exclusive, but not universal: Truth for indigenists is represented by their people and their story, but they have little desire for other groups to either accept or adopt that truth.

From Terry Muck, Harold Netland, and Gerald McDermott, eds., *Handbook of Religion* (Grand Rapids: Baker Academic, 2014), 184.

meeting, the Paris Universal Exposition, which held many congresses devoted to "all the sciences and industries which modern civilization has produced."[19]

The differences were palpable. The Paris Congress was smaller in every way: fewer participants (150), fewer papers (60), less time (five days). But the more important differences lay in the scope of the program and what the participants were asked to do. The Paris Congress was a conference for scholars only. No church bodies were represented, and no popular audiences were there to woo; no creeds were championed. Nathaniel Schmidt summarizes the conference in this way: "It was a meeting of scholars, with scholastic interests, in academic halls, far from the scenes of vital religious conflict and practical endeavor."[20] As Jean Reville, a scholar and the son of conference organizer Albert Reville, puts it, "The rules of the Exposition formally excluded everything that savored in the slightest of politics or creed."[21]

19. Jean Reville, "The International Congress of the History of Religions," *The Open Court* (November 1900): 271.
20. Schmidt, "Paris Congress," 448.
21. Reville, "International Congress," 271.

This approach to an interreligious meeting was not entirely new. A much smaller conference of religion scholars was an annual event in France, and Schmidt notes that three years earlier a larger meeting was held in Stockholm, where a dedication to scientific methods of studying religion was manifest. But the presence of scholars who represented non-Christian religions—and indeed were practitioners of these religions, in addition to being scholarly experts—were far fewer in number at Stockholm than they were at Paris. Perhaps the word *international* in the name of the conference was a shorthand way of conveying this fact.

The intentional limiting of the conference to scholars, particularly those who scientifically studied religion, extended further to a single, preferred research methodology. The only scholarly methodology permitted was historical. The Paris Congress was a history of religions conference, not a social scientific study of religion or a psychology of religion. It wasn't an anthropology of religion or a philosophy of religion; it wasn't even a phenomenological or evolutionary study of religion. Just history. The history of religions was the privileged discipline—all others would need to find (or start) their own meetings. To be sure, one participant (Schmidt) wondered whether they could really discuss "a historic problem without introducing a modicum of philosophical speculation," but by gum, they were going to try.

Did they succeed? And do the meetings that are held once every four years (by the International Association of the History of Religion) since the Paris meeting succeed in excising both dialogue and mission from their meetings? Are the meetings purely scholarly events? I will attempt to restrict myself to the Paris meeting and will respond to the question with a yes-and-no answer that might be summarized thus: even if scholarly method can be isolated from dialogue and mission, the other elements of scholarly research—content, context, scholar, subject, question—most assuredly cannot.

It is debatable whether the triumphalism of French civilization was any less pronounced at this congress than American exceptionalism had been at the parliament seven years earlier. In other words, the French historians of religion felt they were at the apex of civilization: "This worthy Exposition sums up the progress of humanity as the century closes. The traditions of the past in this place impose

obligations of leadership in theological thought; and the present
assumes these obligations by offering more generous opportunities
for the scientific study of the religions of mankind than can be found
anywhere else in the world."[22] So much for leaving out mission.

As for dialogue, there had been explicit criticism of the Stockholm
meeting in terms of the "warm sense of relationships" that pervaded
the atmosphere of the meeting. Apparently, it was an attitude beneath
the seriousness of men devoted to scholarly pursuits. Perhaps the
participants of the Paris Congress felt that it would be well to excise
that kind of relational warmth from their meeting as well. Perhaps.
But here they were again, talking about attitudes and relationships
at the Paris Congress: "No portrayal of nineteenth century civilization would be complete without a suggestion of that unity of spirit
in the midst of diversity of religious beliefs that is now taking the
place of age-long pride, prejudice, and animosity."[23] Goals not entirely scholarly.

Scholars will recognize in this discussion the echo of a very modern
debate over objectivity—or lack thereof—in all scientific and social
scientific work. To what extent is the scholar able to be objective
about his or her work? What role does subjectivity play in the study
of religion? Joachim Wach notes that "the cold grey eyes"[24] of a
religion scholar understand little of value and even less about their
subject matter. In other words, the attempt to dispassionately approach one's study ultimately fails to achieve the Holy Grail of all
academia: understanding. But the converse is also true: understanding
is irretrievably skewed by unaccounted bias, prejudice, and advocacy.

Because of this, scholars of religion have a deep-seated suspicion
of mission, which they see as replacing the pristine goal of "understanding only" with something far more volatile—such as political,
religious, and economic goals of one sort or another. But scholars are
also suspicious of dialogue, which seems to reduce critical thinking
to relational "feel-good-ism." This discomfort persists even when
postmodern scholars point out the different "missions" of various

22. Schmidt, "Paris Congress," 447.
23. Ibid.
24. Joachim Wach, *The Comparative Study of Religion* (New York: Columbia
University Press, 1958), 9.

sciences, as well as the unexpressed presuppositions and assumptions we all bring to every aspect of our lives. It persists even further when allowances for the "relational" are insisted on, that is, the way we are unavoidably affected by the work we do and how others are unavoidably affected by our simple presence.

Make no mistake: the Paris Congress of the History of Religions was different from the World's Parliament of Religions. It was not a forum where participants were invited to make speeches about their religions in the hope of finding sympathetic ears; nor was it a conference where it was acceptable to persuasively argue for the teachings and practices of a religion in the hope of finding new members. Nevertheless, sympathetic ears were present, and they were listening. The scholarly presentations were shot through with persuasive attempts to bring others around to a particular point of view. Thus the complex of elements we are considering—scholarship, mission, and dialogue—are ever present. They are like shape-shifting phantoms, the form and strength of which we are left to find out.

World Missionary Conference, Edinburgh, 1910

The World Missionary Conference took place in Edinburgh, Scotland, from June 14 to June 23, 1910. Protestant mission societies and denominations, mostly from Europe and North America, sent twelve hundred delegates to the meeting, which was held in the Assembly Hall of the United Free Church of Scotland. Some of the delegates were administrators, and others were working missionaries from across the globe. Representation was especially strong from India and Asia and unusually weak from Africa. It was a Protestant conference—no Roman Catholic or Eastern Orthodox missionary organizations were invited. An additional notable lacuna in the delegate representation was the lack of mission organizations and missionaries who ministered to Buddhist populations.[25]

Two goals were stated for the meeting. The first was to deepen the church's sense of its missionary obligations to the world. Although

25. Brian Stanley, *The World Missionary Conference, Edinburgh 1910* (Grand Rapids: Eerdmans, 2009).

the conference was held at what many considered the apex of the Protestant mission effort—at the end of the Great Century of Protestant Missions, as Kenneth Cracknell calls it[26]—much work was left to be done. At that time, only 32 percent of the world's population identified themselves as Christian. Attendees at this meeting were enthusiastic to reach the other two-thirds of the world with the gospel. The second goal was to more clearly identify problems missionaries were facing and to think outside the box when developing methods to reach the unreached. One on-the-scene observer reports:

> The Conference then will concern itself with what has been done; still more with what is going to be done; and most of all with how it may be done. It will endeavor to co-ordinate missionary experience from all parts of the world in order to arrive at a concerted policy as to the wisest plan for distributing gospel agents and agencies, subjecting all existing plans and methods to searching investigation. It will endeavor to be a beginning, not an end. With the greatest missionary age hereto, the nineteenth century, behind us, a fresh start must be made so that the twentieth century may become a yet greater missionary epoch.[27]

In order to accomplish this ambitious task, eight commissions of twenty persons each were assigned two years of preconference work on a specific aspect of the work to be done. Each of the commissions produced a single volume that was circulated to all the delegates before the meeting commenced so that all attendees came ready to interact with work already on the road toward completion. Commission Four, which was assigned the topic "Missionary Message in Relation to the Non-Christian World," has received the most attention by far in the years and decades that followed the conference. A more detailed look at their report and why it has been the focal point of analysis will be discussed later in this chapter.

The Edinburgh mission conference was one conference in a long line of mission conferences before and after 1910. For two reasons, however, it has achieved iconic status as far as worldwide missionary

---

26. Kenneth Cracknell, *Justice, Courtesy, Love: Theologians and Missionaries Encountering World Religions* (London: Epworth, 1995).

27. Ashley Carus-Wilson, "A World Parliament on Missions: The Meaning and Methods of the Edinburgh Conference of 1910," *Quiver* 45 (1910): 631–35.

conferences go. First, the conference is seen by many as the beginning of an ecumenical moment. As David Bebbington observes, "Edinburgh 1910 laid the foundations of interdenominational understanding for the ecumenical movement of the twentieth century."[28] A Continuation Committee was formed in the years following the conference, leading to the establishment of the International Missionary Council in 1921, which in turn led to the formation of the World Council of Churches in 1948.

Second, as the work of Commission Four clearly shows, the World Missionary Conference was a watershed moment in the way Christian mission workers thought of, approached, and treated adherents of other religious traditions. Most of its delegates were captivated in one way or another by what came to be called "fulfillment theology." While many delegates embraced fulfillment theology, many reacted against it. But either way, no one could ignore fulfillment theology, particularly after reading the report of Commission Four. Because fulfillment theology impacts the answer to our question *Why study religion?*, it deserves further comment.

Fulfillment theology is an evolutionary approach to understanding how non-Christian religions relate to Christianity. Put most simply, according to fulfillment theology Christianity is at the top of the evolutionary scale, the ideal that all the rest of religious history tries to attain. Local manifestations of other religions can be seen as way stations along the evolutionary trail; each has glimmers of truth mixed with a great deal of error. The mission task is to identify the glimmers of truth and use them as "points of contact" in an attempt to make the religion in question more proximate to Christianity.

Fulfillment theology lends itself to dialogue in a way that older, more adversarial approaches to people of other religious traditions don't. If a Buddhist I meet, for example, can be encouraged in the glimmers of truth he or she expresses through Buddhist forms, then a conversation can take place, which may develop into a relationship that is positive and affirming rather than judgmental and hell-consigning. Respect is not based simply on the abstract ideal of a person's humanity but on the more explicit, concrete ground of actual religious belief and practice. To make fulfillment theology useful

28. Back cover copy of Stanley, *World Missionary Conference*.

demands a long relational pull in the direction of friendship. The skills of dialogue play a consistent role.

Fulfillment theology, in order to achieve its goals, demands a detailed knowledge of the religions of the people with whom one interacts. It is hard to imagine something like fulfillment theology developing in a climate devoid of religious studies. In such a climate, however, it is the kind of theology that makes sense. As we have seen, the end of the nineteenth century and the beginning of the early twentieth century put the study of "foreign" religions front and center in the great universities of the day. Looking for points of contact meant a fairly sophisticated knowledge of the religion in question.

The Edinburgh mission conference is sometimes seen by more conservative Christians as a move toward the liberal end of the theological spectrum. It wasn't really. Fulfillment theology falls short and has been surpassed, not because it is liberal but because it fails to advance the cause of mission. It is too cerebral and focuses too much on theological and philosophical understandings of religion, which are restricted to the upper echelons of a religious group or sometimes not evident at all. It is too dependent on context for meaning—in some places it is easy to identify points of contact with Christianity, and in other contexts it is almost impossible.

Edinburgh was a missionary conference, but its approach to mission was different and new. It attempted to take into account the new emphases of dialogue and relationality that the World's Parliament of Religions in Chicago had set in motion in regard to the birth of twentieth-century Christian identity. What's more, the World Missionary Conference fully endorsed the new science of religion as a necessary arrow in the quiver of missional methods and preparation. All three methods—the scholarly, the missional, and the dialogical—became fixtures of Western identity in the one hundred years since these three watershed meetings took place.

A Delightful Complexity

If Max Müller was the father of religious studies—the public champion for the scientific study of religion presiding from his station as

professor of comparative philology at Oxford University—then James
Legge was its silent uncle. After several decades of mission work in
Hong Kong and China, Legge "retired" to Oxford as professor of
Chinese language and literature. He was "convinced of the need for
missionaries to be able to comprehend the ideas and culture of the
Chinese" and thus in 1841 began the long task of translating the
Confucian Classics into English.[29] Before he was finished he had not
only translated the "official" classics but also many other important
books of religious philosophy and Chinese literature. To accomplish
this task, he arose every day at three o'clock in the morning, drank
one cup of tea, and set to work. Every day. For twenty years.[30]

The books Legge translated, especially the Confucian Classics,
are still being used by scholars of Chinese religion around the world.
Some of these translated classics were published in his five-volume
work, *The Chinese Classics*.[31] Others were crucial to the success of
Müller's monumental Sacred Books of the East series, a fifty-volume
set of translations of Eastern religious works. In addition, Legge
wrote books about Chinese religion, such as *The Religions of China*,
The Life and Teachings of Confucius, and *The Life and Teachings of
Mencius*, which are still read widely by scholars of Chinese religion.
That being the case, Legge was a religious studies scholar, right? One
of the greatest ever, by all accounts?

Well, yes and no. He was a missionary first and never really re-
nounced that calling. What's more, he was explicit in saying that his
translation work was done for the benefit of missionaries in China.
Yet if given the choice between identifying himself as a scholar, a
missionary, or even a person interested in building better relationships with the Chinese people, I wonder what his answer might have
been. He did what scholars do—he published classic books and gave
lectures to students. He did what missionaries do—he was president
of a college in Hong Kong and pastored a church there for years.

29. Norman Girardot, *The Victorian Translation of China: James Legge's Oriental
Pilgrimage* (Berkeley: University of California Press, 2002), 225.

30. Ibid., 357.

31. James Legge, *The Chinese Classics*, 5 vols. (Oxford: Clarendon, 1893). Includes
The Life and Teachings of Confucius, The Life and Teachings of Mencius, and *The
Religions of China*.

And he did what people interested in interreligious dialogue do—he interacted with people of other religions. One of his conditions for accepting an appointment at Oxford was that he could bring students from China with him to seek Oxford degrees.

In an important way, the complexities of Legge's interreligious vocation and the difficulties we have in describing it are paradigmatic of the mixed feelings many if not most of us at the beginning of the twenty-first century experience in relationship to non-Christian religions. We are uncertain about what Christian mission to other religions means, and even if we eschew that explicit mission entirely, a little psychological excavation unearths a great many other "missions" just beneath the surface. We are convinced of the importance of relating well to people of other religions, even if we disagree on specific questions of religious fact and value, yet what do we do with the feelings produced by the conviction that our religion is the best one? Studying religion just makes good common sense. It satisfies curiosities, to be sure, but it also communicates well-deserved respect of other people's deeply held beliefs.

Like it or not, we are heirs to the parliament of 1893, the congress of 1900, and the conference of 1910. Each of these meetings and the movements they unleashed have developed and changed in the past one hundred years, but each is represented in our individual and communal psyches. But how do we account for all three movements, especially when the way in which they are typically presented and championed often makes it seem like they are irreconcilable? Honestly, there may not be a single formula to accomplish this task, no simple way to combine them in the twenty-first-century identity.

Why would we want to develop a formula approach to their combination? All three are present in our psyches, but what makes the question interesting is the different ways in which people and groups put them together. It turns out to be a delightful complexity, the nature of which turns on the differences in inherited personality, religious tradition, vocational choice, and other factors. When it comes to each of our individual interreligious identities, let a thousand flowers bloom.

I close with two conclusions. First, all three historic meetings are present to some degree and in some form in our Western cultural identity. Embrace that fact and see where it leads. Second, consider the statement of that fact to be one part of the answer to the question of this book. If an important part of the modern Western interreligious identity is the scholarly study of religion, then that in itself is a reason to recognize it in the behaviors associated with the teaching and learning about religions—not only our own religion but also the other religions of the world.

Why I Study Religion

FRANCES S. ADENEY, LOUISVILLE SEMINARY

I suppose my interest in religions began as a very young child. I experienced the tantalizing aromas of Mrs. Friedman's kosher food simmering in her kitchen on the other side of our rented duplex when I was three or four. I remember the walk to the tall-steepled Lutheran church down the highway where my big brother went to kindergarten. Only I among my siblings volunteered to go to 6 a.m. mass with my paternal grandmother when we visited her in the big city of Passaic, New Jersey. The frigid walks ended at the Roman Catholic Church where grandma got busy with her rosary and I was free to stare at the ornate statues of the crucifix and the Virgin Mary. I was awestruck.

When I was about six years old my mother discovered what Garrison Keillor called "the sanctified brethren." We began worshiping at Harold and Leila Crane's home up the lane from our new house in Summerville, New Jersey. From underneath the grand piano I could see the rays of the sun alight on the "elements," the bread and wine of communion or, as we called it, the "breaking of bread." The unveiling of the bread and wine from underneath a white napkin occurred at 11:50 a.m., nearly one hour after the mostly silent service began. An old man, usually Mr. Ross, would pray and pass the bread and wine to the eligible grown-ups. Of course I was not allowed. This event too was awesome.

At this stage, I began to note differences among the religions. Roman Catholics were anathema to my parents, who were both from Catholic families. Yet my Catholic cousins, aunts, and grandmother all seemed happy with their religion. I read *Pilgrim's Progress* in grade school, so I knew how bad the Roman Church was. The Plymouth Brethren (Grant-Kelly Exclusive Brethren Number 8, according to the US government) also emphasized the evils of Catholicism. At the same time, my mother often shopped at the St. Vincent DePaul's secondhand store to clothe her swiftly growing family. I purchased books to read there, many of which had Catholic messages for young readers. I soon set up a little altar on my dresser. The simple cross wasn't quite the crucifix or the Virgin Mary, but the flowers helped. This became a holy spot for me.

As a devout Brethren teenager I read the books of J. N. Darby and went to the women's prayer meetings at the Iowa Conference while my teenage friends found other things to do. At the same time, I went to prom and had a high-school sweetheart, much to my parents' dismay.

I became seriously interested in the study of religion when my three children were growing up. I began to research new religious movements to see how Eastern religions intersected with religions of the West. My first article, published in *The New Age Rage,* critiques transpersonal psychology from a Christian perspective. As research director of the Spiritual Counterfeits Project, I put together a journal titled *The Flowering of the Human Potential Movement.* I soon realized that my knowledge of both American culture and religions other than my own was dangerously lacking.

As a result, I applied to the Graduate Theological Union's joint program with the University of California at Berkeley to study the sociology of religion. So began my academic study of religion—a study I still avidly pursue thirty years later.

5

Clashing Religions

Contestation, Consilience, Confession

If societies are changing, bringing about corresponding changes in specifically religious societies, and if individuals are becoming more complex in terms of religious identity and meaning, then what can be said about the religions themselves? First of all, religions are not passive recipients of the effects of societal change and individual complexity. Religions are change agents in their own right. In addition to being affected by changes going on around them, religions are making decisions about their own policies and behaviors that in turn affect cultures and people. In other words, the relationship between society and religion is reciprocal. Having described what is happening outside the religions and how that might be affecting not only the religions but also our study of them, the same approach must be applied to what is going on inside the religions and how that might be affecting societies and cultures in general. Alternatively, how might religions want to change societies and individuals? These insights might reveal areas of research important for religious studies scholars, young and old alike.

That being said, "What is going on inside the religions?" is a rather big category to tackle. To bring it in line with the specific goal of this book, to make a case for why studying religion is important, I have limited the discussion to what is going on inside the religions in terms of their relationships with other religions. Interreligious relationships, after all, are one of the things a scholar of religion must account for, if not study specifically. By learning about interreligious relationships we also learn about the effects of religion in general on the societies and cultures in which they exist. I would like to begin this chapter with a story.

During the 1990s, I edited *Christianity Today* magazine. Our offices were in Carol Stream, Illinois, and on many days it was a hectic job. Although I loved the work, I felt the need to occasionally get away from it all. I needed a retreat geographically close to Christianity Today Inc. where I could be anonymous.

Three-tenths of a mile down Schmale Road was the American headquarters of the Theosophical Society. It sits on a multi-acre estate, in the center of which sits Olcott Hall, which is named after the first president of the Theosophical Society, Henry Steel Olcott. At one end of Olcott Hall is the headquarters' theosophical library.

It is a small library with wood-paneled walls and high bookcases filled with books on religion. It is quiet. Quite frankly, not a lot of Wheaton, Illinois, residents belong to the Theosophical Society. And of those who do, my guess is that few of them read *Christianity Today* magazine. Thus it was the perfect retreat for me. I sat in a huge stuffed chair, unmolested, as I read and thought to my heart's content.

I thought of that experience as I sat down to write this chapter on clashing religions. By "clashing" I mean to convey that we live in a world where different religions increasingly come in contact with one another in public places, in scholars' studies, at business workplaces, during political negotiations, and increasingly in the everyday lives of people.

The word *clash* is not meant to convey that these interreligious events are all negative. Some are, of course. But many, if not most, are innocuous encounters among friends and families in neighborhoods that used to be 90 percent Christian but are now only 50 percent Christian. Not only are many such encounters innocuous, but often the two people clashing don't even acknowledge that contact is taking place—such as my "clash" with the Theosophical Society twenty years ago. I sat in their library, and they let me sit there.

Such contacts, once relatively anonymous and impersonal, are becoming increasingly public, acknowledged, and consequential. They make a difference, and because they make a difference, we need to acknowledge them. For Western scholars of religion it is a dynamic that cannot be ignored; it affects everything. For many scholars the clash, whatever forms it takes, becomes the occasion for and subject of their research projects. Taking a look at some of the examples of the overall cultural clash, three categories emerge: clashes leading to contestation, clashes in which the goal is consilience, and clashes that originate with confession.

First, let's ask where my particular clash with the Theosophical Society might fall on a spectrum of contestation, consilience, and confession. Perhaps it has some elements of all three:

- It could be an example of peaceful coexistence, which often characterizes the way religious groups in Western cultures interact. I was welcomed at the Theosophical Society, and I in turn welcomed the solace their library offered me.

- However, this clash could be seen as emblematic of the differences that exist among the religions and how those differences can sometimes lead to problems. As the editor of a conservative Christian magazine, I might be seen as a competitor with those in the Theosophical Society, and vice versa.

- Whether or not we acknowledge it, exchanges of religious content, ideals, and practices do take place in these clashes, though we may not know to what end.

In an attempt to make the results of all three outcomes more clear (let's call them moments of interreligious interchange), I will look at each in turn.

In some senses, the clashing of the religions is a relatively new phenomenon. At the very least, it is taking a new form. The existence of religious plural societies in which more than one of the major religions exists de facto is not the new feature, although multireligious societies are a step removed from tribal and archaic groups in which religion itself is not a separate category of identification. What is new about religiously plural societies is that one of the religions does not necessarily receive preferential treatment (theoretically at least). In the past, one religion might have been the favorite of the ruling power, party, or person in cultures where more than one major religion existed. Or perhaps one of the religions was "established," meaning that it received political endorsement that usually included financial incentives.

Today more and more religiously plural cultures are *democratic* religiously plural cultures, meaning that freedom of religion—usually accompanied by some form of separation of church/mosque/synagogue/temple and state—is the law of the land. The United States Constitution was the first official political pronouncement of this kind of relationship between religions and societies, although one can see glimmers of it in previous political systems. The great Indian king Asoka, for example, became a staunch Buddhist but still advocated freedom of religion for all of his subjects. Today this type of religious freedom is not the exception but the ideal, championed by the United Nations Declaration of Human Rights.[1] This is not to say that religious pluralism dominates the world political scene, however. The Islamic world has not fully come to terms with this approach to religious pluralism, and, in a slightly different way, China has yet to fully embrace it.

In this chapter I focus more on the religions themselves, looking both phenomenologically and historically at the way in which the mighty clash of the religions has played itself out. The patterns of the clash have not been consistent. In some cases the clash has led to harmony and peaceful coexistence, but in other examples it has led to confrontation—sometimes violent confrontation. In both cases the attempt has been to allow the religions to be themselves, even as they face other religious forces whose concepts of "being themselves"

---

1. Frances Adeney and Arvind Sharma, *Christianity and Human Rights* (Albany: State University of New York Press, 2007).

involve trying to determine what the other religions should be. Let's look at each of these examples in turn. In the process, I will point out some of the ways in which the clash, whatever form it takes, affects how and why we study religion.

Contestation

Most of us are conditioned to think that the roots of religious contestation—confrontations and conflicts—lie in disagreements over competing religious truths. However, this is probably not the case. If the sociobiologist nonpareil E. O. Wilson is even close to being right, the drive to contest and confront is genetic in origin. In answer to the question as to whether human beings are innately aggressive toward one another, Wilson answers yes: "Innateness refers to the measurable probability that a trait will develop in a specified set of environments, not to the certainty that the trait will develop in all environments. By this criterion human beings have a marked hereditary predisposition to aggressive behavior."[2]

Being a good scientist, Wilson gets specific. He goes on to enumerate seven different aggressive behaviors that are hardwired into our nervous systems: "defense and conquest of territory, assertion of dominance within well-organized groups, sexual aggression, acts of hostility by which weaning is terminated, aggression against prey, defensive counterattacks against predators, and moralistic and disciplinary aggression used to enforce the rules of society."[3]

The implications of this biological observation for religion are clear. As innately aggressive animals, we human beings are predisposed to confront one another with the religious ideas we hold personally and communally. Since this is our nature, there is probably little we can do to change the fact that contestations among the religions will take place. But scholars can still study the nature of these contests. Although such study is oriented to description, the societal implications of their findings are never difficult to discern.

2. E. O. Wilson, *On Human Nature* (Cambridge, MA: Harvard University Press, 1978), 101.
3. Ibid., 102.

▌ STUDY AID

RELIGION AND VIOLENCE EXERCISE

1. Make the best argument you can for each of the following statements.

   Throughout history, religion has provided humans with the most egregious motivation to do violence to fellow human beings.

   Throughout history, religion has provided human beings with the most powerful motivations to work for peace for all humankind.

   In your argument for each, make the case as if you believed it, even though they are contradictory and/or you may think they are incomplete as stated. For each statement, indicate which authorities, both ancient and modern, you would cite to defend your argument.

2. Write your own statement of how you think religion, violence, and peace interrelate with one another.

3. How might a Christian statement of the relationship between religion and peace compare and contrast with some other religion's statement(s)?

From Terry Muck, Harold Netland, and Gerald McDermott, eds., *Handbook of Religion* (Grand Rapids: Baker Academic, 2014), 769.

Consider, as examples, two religious studies scholars—Max Weber and Mark Juergensmeyer—who have done work on the contests that take place among the religions.

Weber was a German sociologist, philosopher, and sociologist of religion. Along with Émile Durkheim and Karl Marx, he is credited with founding the modern scholarly discipline of sociology. All three scholars spent a great deal of their research energies on discerning how religion influences societal form and development, whether for good (Weber and Durkheim) or for ill (Marx). Each made distinctive contributions.

One of Weber's major interests involves the dynamics of how religions spread. In particular, when a religion comes in contact with a new culture and its existing religion, what factors determine whether that religion takes root in that new culture and thrives or, like a seed falling on rocky soil, eventually withers and dies? In this regard, one of Weber's ideas is that climate has a great deal of influence on the types of religion that prosper—that is, certain types of religion thrive in arid, rocky, and desert climates, and other types of religion thrive in fertile, wooded, and jungle environments. While an interesting set of theses, this theory is not supported by a great deal of empirical data and is largely ignored by scholars today.

Another of Weber's ideas, however—something he calls "elective affinity"—still provides insights to sociologists of religion in their analyses.[4] Elective affinity teaches that certain types of religions have teachings and practices that find more resonances with certain types of social and cultural patterns than they do with other social and cultural patterns. When a migrating religion comes in contact with a culture with which it has affinity, it tends to flourish, while contact with radically different cultural forms almost ensures that the religion will develop only a marginal presence in that culture—or may not survive at all.

In particular, when today's scholars of Buddhism, Christianity, and Islam (known as the "missionary" religions) look at the history and spread of these religions from their cultural homes in India and the Middle East, they tend to use some of Weber's ideas regarding elective affinity. Weber's most influential book in this regard is *The Protestant Ethic and the Spirit of Capitalism*,[5] the thesis of which is that Protestant Christianity flourished in the West in capitalistic countries because of religious and cultural affinity based on economics.

As both major and minor religions continue to grow and spread in today's world, an understanding of what leads to spread, growth, and flourishing, as well as what leads to stagnation and decline, will become increasingly important. This is a topic that religions study about themselves in some detail in order to make their mission efforts more effective. However, it is also a topic that begs for the approaches used by religious studies scholars in order to discern patterns across the religions.

Mark Juergensmeyer, a scholar of religion who teaches at the University of California, Santa Barbara, has devoted great scholarly energy to studying religious violence. While Weber studied the contest

4. Max Weber, "The Social Psychology of the World Religions," in *From Max Weber: Essays in Sociology*, ed. H. H. Gerth and C. Wright Mills (New York: Oxford University Press, 1946), 284–85.

5. Max Weber, *The Protestant Ethic and the Spirit of Capitalism* (New York: Penguin Books, 2002).

of religions at their best, Juergensmeyer's work tends to see them at their worst, particularly when they resort (or are forced to resort) to violence in order to survive, grow, and spread. His interest in the study of religious violence stems from a couple of years he spent in the Punjab. Juergensmeyer lived among Sikhs who, ironically, are known for being warm, opened-hearted, and generous; they follow a peaceful spiritual teaching that emphasizes the egalitarian ethos of the community. As he puts it, "When an awful spiral of violence began to emerge in the Punjab in the 1980s, between the Indian government and the rural Sikh youth, I wanted to know why."[6] His scholarly writings follow this theme, and perhaps his best-known work is the Grauwmeyer award-winning book *Terror in the Mind of God*.[7]

The questions raised by the contestation of religions cannot be answered by simply saying that religions should not enter into contests of one sort or another with other religions. History, biology, and social science all clearly indicate that this goal is impossible. What may be possible, however, is a differentiation between negative, harmful contestation and contestation carried out with full respect and honor for all religions. Interreligious violence falls in the first category while peaceful dialogue and debate falls in the second. Given the current world religion scene, which has more than its share of negative contestation, this is a fruitful area of research for a young religious studies scholar to take up.

Consilience

Whereas contestation emphasizes the individuality and particularity of each religion, consilience emphasizes the universality of each, that is, the things the religions tend to have in common. Scholars are good at making these distinctions. The categorization of the animal kingdom (which is one of six kingdoms, the other five being plants, fungi, protists, monerans, and archaea) into phyla, families, species,

6. See Juergensmeyer's short testimony, "Why I Study Religion," at the end of chapter 1 of this book.

7. Mark Juergensmeyer, *Terror in the Mind of God: The Global Rise of Religious Violence* (Berkeley: University of California Press, 1999).

and genera is a great example.[8] Sociologists of religion find such categorizations especially useful in their work. For instance, Weber's distinctions among different kinds of world religions, particularly between world-affirming religions and world-denying religions, are used by sociologists of religion everywhere.

What is consilience? *Consilience* (in historical and scientific studies) refers to a widely accepted principle that "truth" is consistent across cultural, temporal, geographical, and methodological boundaries. If evidence from those different spheres converges in common conclusions, then conclusions regarding the phenomenon being studied are stronger than if each finding in each sphere is considered separately. Consilience does not deny difference across spheres; indeed, it assumes cultural, temporal, and geographic difference. Yet it posits that when common results emerge across lines of acknowledged difference, the results are even more powerful because of, not in spite of, the differences.

How might the concept of consilience relate to the worlds of human religiosity? In much the same way as it does in history and science. When religions find areas of agreement across lines of difference, those findings should be considered powerful. They should not, I would like to emphasize, be seen as either some sort of religious perennialism or as a kind of negative endorsement of religious relativism and incommensurability. For example, the fact that religious behavior seems almost universal across all of human history, both temporal and geographical, is a powerful example of consilience regarding the conclusion that religion is a universal human behavior, a part of human nature.

The religious studies scholar who has done the most to point up the great areas of consilience among the religious peoples of the world is Wilfred Cantwell Smith (1916–2000).[9] Smith's field was comparative religion. He was born in Canada and taught at the University of Toronto and McGill University in Montreal; he also taught in the United States from 1964 to 1973, as director of Harvard's Center for the Study of the World's Religions.

8. E. O. Wilson, "The Ionian Enchantment," in *Consilience* (New York: Vintage, 1998), 3–14.
9. There is no major biography of Smith and his work. He deserves one.

Smith's scholarly work challenges the very concept of religion, if by religion one means the discrete, classified religions, such as world religions (Hinduism, Buddhism, Islam, Christianity, etc.), indigenous religions (Celtic religion, Native American religions, African tribal religions), and new religious movements (Hare Krishna, Soka Gakkai, Mormonism, etc.). For Smith, such divisions obscure the central fact that all human beings are religious and each individual has his or her own version of faith—faith being the primary category of religion. The clearest statement of this position is Smith's classic work *The Meaning and End of Religion*.[10]

Smith, of course, does not deny that the specific religions exist. He simply argues that these are primarily historical and contextual accommodations, that none of the religious founders (with the possible exception of Muhammad) intended to begin a "religion" per se, and that "faith" is a far better category of research than "religion" for the scholar of religion to pursue. By making the faith of men and women the category of study, Smith finds consilience in the findings of a host of cross-religion categories, including scripture, belief, and theology, and he wrote major works on all three (*What Is Scripture?*, *Faith and Belief*, and *Towards a World Theology*).

Let me be clear about what Smith's position is *not* saying.

All religions are the same. Just because we share the same story of human religiosity does not mean that all of our stories are the same. Each of us, both individually and communally, has a specific role to play in the grand narrative of human religiosity. While all roles are part of the same plot, each role can be vastly different from the other roles.

All religions are true. As with any great story, not all the elements of the story are of equal value when it comes to truth. Some parts of any story may be more true than other parts. Some roles are more consistent with the overall message of the story than other roles. Some events move the story along toward its apparent conclusion, while others block that movement or even cause it to regress.

All religions are good. Similarly, not all the elements of the story are good. Every story has its villains, who personify evil. Every story

---

10. Wilfred Cantwell Smith, *The Meaning and End of Religion: A New Approach to the Religious Traditions of Mankind* (New York: Macmillan, 1962).

has its disasters, which in their overall effect seem to glorify evil. It is up to both the reader and the other actors in the story to discern which is which.

Smith's position can be summarized by saying that humankind's religious history is best understood and studied as one single narrative with many, many different stories and subplots that are derived from the single narrative thread—rather like a *Mahabharata* for all humanity or a *Ramayana* for more than just Indians and South Asians. We gain far more, Smith argues, from viewing religion this way than we do from considering religions as being isolated in watertight compartments, almost incommensurable with one another. In addition to increased understanding, we gain a community of faith-seekers across historical and cultural differences.

Smith's thesis is controversial both to scholars of religion and to adherents of specific religions who want to view their religious story as the one true and unique story, not just a subplot of a larger human religious narrative. But Smith raises an issue that is important. The enduring popularity of *The Meaning and End of Religion* seems to indicate that most of humanity is torn when it comes to evaluating religion, both one's own religion and the religions of one's neighbors. People are torn between pride in their own faith and their recognition of the similarities their faith has with the religions of others. Thus scholars of religion have much to contribute in the way of data and observation as humanity struggles to understand these complementary urges.

Confession

The final way to look at the clash among religions is to examine them from the point of view of confession, that is, by the way in which each religion looks to individual religious peoples on their own religious journeys. This is not the point of view of consilience, which posits some grand, overarching narrative that looks for enduring cross-religious patterns. Nor it is the point of view of contestation, the positive and negative interactions among religions and religious peoples, which fuels the dynamic of human history. Confession is the accumulation of individual religious stories of people of all religions the world over.

Why call it *confession* though? It seems a misuse of the word as we know it. When we think of confession we usually think of a person verbally acknowledging his or her misdeeds or sins. We most often associate it with a court of law, where the word *confession* has an almost technical meaning; in this sense, confession is something a guilty person does to give voice to his or her crimes or shortcomings. Usually we "confess" after the evidence against us begins to pile up, that is, when it is plain to all that we are guilty.

But there is another sense of this word. In Christian circles, *confession* has often meant the statement—written, spoken, or implied—of what it is we believe. One of the greatest of all the church's theologians, Augustine, wrote a classic book called simply *Confessions*.[11] It is a statement of Augustine's spiritual journey, and while it does include some "confession" in the legal sense, its overall form is a witness to what God has done in his life. Similarly, the great Russian novelist Leo Tolstoy wrote a much shorter work called *A Confession*,[12] which is his testimony concerning his beliefs when it comes to spiritual matters. Sometimes when the act of confession is used in this sense, the Latin word *credo* is used in its stead, and *credo* is sometimes translated simply as "I believe."

Religions other than Christianity have similar works. As a young man I was profoundly influenced by reading Mahatma Gandhi's autobiographical work, *The Story of My Experiment with Truth*.[13] Confucius's *Analects* is not only a restatement of traditional Chinese moral teachings but also a revelation of Confucius—who he was and what he believed.[14] Al Ghazali, the greatest of Muslim theologians, wrote a credo called *Deliverance from Error*.[15] Christian theologian H. Richard Niebuhr argues that all revelation is confessional.[16]

11. Augustine, *Confessions*, trans. R. S. Pine-Coffin (Harmondsworth, UK: Penguin Books, 1961).

12. Leo Tolstoy, *A Confession*, trans. Aylmer Maude (Mineola, NY: Dover, 2005).

13. Mahatma Gandhi, *The Story of My Experiment with Truth* (Boston: Beacon, 1993).

14. Confucius, *The Analects*, trans. D. C. Lau (New York: Penguin Books, 1979).

15. Al Ghazali, *Deliverance from Error* (Louisville: Fons Vitae, 2004).

16. H. Richard Niebuhr, *The Meaning of Revelation* (New York: Macmillan, 1960), 62.

At first glance, it may appear that religious confession is the last thing a scholar would want to study. When we say *confession*, we seem to be talking about something a theologian or a Buddhologian or an Islamic mullah is interested in, not something a social scientist gravitates toward. Religious scientists want collections of observable facts, not spiritual ruminations of the sort I have been discussing. Scientists of religion want to study "natural religion," not the existential musings of religious peoples, even if they are the heroes of one's faith. So one might think.

Yet to do so would be to miss an important point about what religious studies is and what religious scholars do. While it is true that they avoid commenting on the truth or falsehood of supernatural religious phenomenon, the phenomenon themselves are studied as expressions of human religious behavior and are considered evidence of the kind of religion being embraced. Likewise, human religious experience and expressions of that experience are fair game for the religious studies scholar as observations of measurable behavior. One can study prayer, for example, without praying or endorsing prayer.

One of the foremost scholars of religion, psychologist of religion William James, contributed enormously to the field of religious studies through his evenhanded collection of individual religious data, as expressed by individual human religious actors in their religious experiences. James did this by taking the mode of religious confession seriously. To be sure, his work also recognizes the mode of contestation: "Everyone is nevertheless prone to claim that his conclusions are the only logical ones in that they are necessities of universal reason, they being all the while, at bottom, accidents more or less of personal vision which had far better be avowed as such."[17] Underlying contestation, James recognizes consilience and begs his readers to recognize it as well, in order to mute the unavoidable bluntness of contestation: "All such differences are minor matters which ought to be subordinated in view of the fact that, whether we be empiricists or rationalists, we are, ourselves, parts of the universe and share the same one deep concern in its destinies."[18] Yet in his

17. William James, *A Pluralistic Universe* (Rockville, MD: Manor, 2008), 10.
18. Ibid., 11.

work James embraces an empiricism that posits the pluralism of the world, which teaches the whole can be known only (if at all) by its parts, and that one collects empirical data through what we are calling "confession" since "a man's vision is *the* great fact about him."[19] James rejects monism, theistic dualism, and absolutism in favor of collecting confessions—individual stories as they are written, spoken, or acted—which are revealed through even the simplest everyday behaviors:

> Whereas absolutism thinks that the said substance becomes fully divine only in the form of totality, and is not its real self in any form but the *all-form*, the pluralistic view which I prefer to adopt is willing to believe that there may ultimately never be an *all-form* at all, that the substance of reality may never get totally collected, that some of it may remain outside of the largest combination of it ever made, and that a distributive form of reality, the *each-form,* is logically as acceptable and empirically as probable as the *all-form*.[20]

James parlayed this empirical, pluralist view of the world and research methodology of the world into a fruitful scholarly career, writing substantive works on philosophy, psychology, and religious studies. As I mentioned earlier, his *Varieties of Religious Experience* (1902) is a classic of American psychology of religion that came about as a result of "hearing confessions" (in the religious studies sense).

Conclusion

Although studying the clash of religions includes many historical dimensions, there is no field of study more hardwired into current events than religious studies. A quick perusal of a newspaper that covers world news quickly reveals the clash of religions worldwide: Hindus, Muslims, and Sikhs clashing in Northwest India; Christians, Jews, and Muslims clashing in the Middle East; Muslims, Christians, and Traditional Religions clashing in Africa; Orthodox Christians, Catholic Christians, and Protestant Christians clashing in Russia—the list

19. Ibid., 14 (emphasis added).
20. Ibid., 19 (emphasis added).

goes on and on. A much shorter list could be made of places where a newsworthy clash of religions is *not* taking place.

Of course, these notable worldwide events *should* receive coverage. Journalists recount the stories and daily events with as much exactitude as they can manage, and the religions tell their respective sides of the stories with increasing media savvy, including the use of print and electronic media and social media. But religious studies scholars bring a perspective to world news that neither journalists nor religions can—or want—to offer. Religious studies scholars tell the rest of the story: how historical backgrounds have brought us to this place and time; how an understanding of different religious belief systems can almost predict what might happen under a given set of conditions; and how empirical, ethnographic studies can save us from the prejudices and biases of profit-based news outlets and religious groups.

Speaking of evidence, let's consider a few examples of religious stories happening right now that beg for scholarly examination—one from each of the three modes of thought: contestation, consilience, and confession.

Contestation

There is perhaps no better exemplar of contestation than the negative example of the Islamic State.[21] A Salafi Jihadi militant group, the Islamic State (as of March 2015) has control over territory in Iraq and Syria, occupied by ten million people. The group wants to spread the religion of Islam and is willing to use extreme physical violence to do so. Many, if not most, of the world's Muslims reject the Islamic State as a true religious group that represents the teachings of Muhammad. But the attempts of Muslims to distance themselves from the Islamic State are difficult to make stick in the minds of people

21. Also called the Islamic State of Iraq and the Levant (ISIL), the Islamic State of Iraq and Syria, and the Islamic State of Iraq and ash-Sham (ISIS). All these designations are controversial, even the shortened and most commonly used name, Islamic State. Most Muslims around the world object to the use of the word *Islamic* in the title, not wanting to be identified with the group's barbarity. As a result, many people are beginning to make the point of referring to the group as Daesh, the acronym of its Arabic name (al-Dawla al-Islamiya fi al-Iraq wa al-Sham). They judge the group to be unrepresentative of true Islam, which raises a question about the general religious studies principle of trying, whenever possible, to let people identify themselves with their preferred terms.

around the world who read of the atrocities carried out almost weekly in the name of the Prophet and his teachings. (Consider the parallel problem Christianity faces in distancing itself from the political excesses of the Crusades and colonialism.) Since such stories are the mother's milk of journalists the world over, the Islamic State rather than peace-loving Muslims receives the publicity. Scholars can help remedy this by providing the history, beliefs, and practices of both the Islamic State and the rest of the worldwide Muslim community.

Consilience

In today's world, one of the biggest stories centers on groups, both large and small, that promote the category of human behavior we call religious. These groups encourage the religions to work together for good in promoting education and relieving human suffering, whether that suffering involves poverty, disease, or injustice. While many such groups exist, I would like to consider the United Religions Initiative (URI). Using a mode of religious engagement that they call "appreciative inquiry," URI strives "to encourage religions to stop fighting, to make peace with one another, and to build together a world of peace, justice, and healing."[22] "Appreciative inquiry" is a method of developing organizations around "the simple and profound act of appreciation" rather than around challenge and confrontation.[23] This method recognizes the good in people and their religions, rather than focusing on the bad, and builds on the consiliences among the religions. As a movement, the URI has achieved enough success that it deserves a scholarly examination of its history, beliefs, and practices—scholarship that will provide the data for religious leaders around the world to make decisions as to whether such movements deserve replication.

Confession

An interesting way to study the current state of religious confession—both its prevalence and the way it is received by people around

22. Charles Gibbs and Sally Mahe, *Birth of a Global Community: Appreciative Inquiry in Action* (Bedford Heights, OH: Lakeshore, 2004), 2.
  23. Ibid.

the world—might be a comparative study detailing the development of religious confession itself: from Augustine of Hippo writing his *Confessions* in fifth-century North Africa, to Leo Tolstoy writing *A Confession* in nineteenth-century Russia, to the use of Facebook by 1.4 billion people to express their personal news, opinions, and angst (some of which is religious). It would be interesting for scholars of the early church to estimate how many people of that era actually had the chance and the skills to read Augustine's work, in a time long before the invention of the printing press and the development of mass literacy. That information could then be compared with the growing literacy of Tolstoy's day and then with the almost unbelievable spread of Facebook across geographical and cultural boundaries. How did these three ways of "confessing" change the way the exchange of religious beliefs and ideas has been received? Indeed, how did they change the forms of the confessions themselves and the ways in which scholars understand them?

All these stories get press, and each benefits from its own press release. In this day and age, promotion of anything is just a click away. But each story demands scholarly examination of the sort I am presenting in this book. There has never been a more exciting time to be a religious studies scholar.

Why I Study Religion

SALLIE B. KING, JAMES MADISON UNIVERSITY

Like most young people, before college I had never heard of studying religion academically, much less imagined going into academic religion studies as a profession. My reasons for choosing such a life, as I see them now, are as follows.

1. I have been thinking about religious questions since childhood. My memories of even early childhood include me frequently puzzling about whether heaven and/or hell exist, why there is so much suffering in the world, how a loving God could possibly condemn people to hell for believing in a different religion, and so on. When it came time to decide

on a career path, I decided that since I would be putting many or most of my waking hours into working, it would be great if I could earn my living by thinking about what I think about all the time anyway.

2. As I got deeper and deeper into my collegiate study of religion, I discovered that religious studies was more satisfying to me intellectually than other fields. I was studying philosophy as well as religion, but I quickly came to feel that religion went both deeper and wider than philosophy. Philosophy assumes the correctness of its rational way of examining questions. This kind of rationality, while extremely powerful and useful, simply cannot answer all questions. In contrast, religious studies is a field rather than a single discipline and thus has the strength of drawing on many disciplinary methodologies—philosophy, psychology, anthropology, sociology, history, art history, textual study, artifact study, living religions study, and many others. Any approach one chooses to take in examining the phenomena of religion can be supplemented and challenged by other approaches, generating endless questions, possibilities, and occasions for self-examination. And since religious studies examines religious phenomena from all times, places, and cultures, one is less likely to see the culturally specific as universal.

As a specialist in Buddhist studies, I appreciate the way that the study of a non-Western religion makes clear to me the religion of my youth. I am not rejecting the way of thinking with which I was raised, but because of my studies I can live, intellectually, in more than one world. I can see things through my Euro-American Christian eyes, generating and processing ideas and concepts in the terms of Euro-American Christian culture, and I can do the same with and through Buddhist eyes. I can look at any subject first in one way and then in another. This allows me to see the relativity of each culture's conceptual constructs, their strengths and weaknesses, and what is and is not possible to think within those terms. This is eye opening. I wish everyone could have such an experience.

3. Finally, the other factor in my deciding to pursue religious studies was my lifelong concern for the suffering of the world. I went to college thinking that I would pursue a career in foreign service, helping shape US foreign policy. But that approach didn't go nearly deep enough. In a democracy, I reasoned, the government's behavior ultimately is an extension of the will of the people. Taking a kind of "think globally, act locally" approach, I decided that I wanted to focus my efforts on addressing the deep values and attitudes of my students who, as American citizens, would shape the actions of the most powerful country in the world. I wanted to help them learn about and come to respect other cultures, to share with them the greatest ideals known to humankind, and to encourage them not only to think carefully about their own values but also to live up to their own ideals.

In this way, studying, teaching, and engaging in scholarship in academic religious studies has allowed me simultaneously to pursue my deepest and most challenging intellectual curiosity and to serve humankind in a way that I hope will help reduce human suffering.

PART 3

HOW?

One of the first questions that should occur to those taking on a new quest is *What kind of skills do I need?* After the initial excitement of the decision wears off, the student begins to wonder what it is they have gotten themselves into. A bit of doubt begins to creep into their mind as they assess whether they think they can do this; if they decide they can, they wonder how much work the endeavor is going to take. Chapters 6, 7, and 8 tackle these "how" questions of religious studies.

Chapter 6 introduces the three most basic skills a student of religion needs: (1) how to study religious texts; (2) how to talk to religious people; and (3) how to compare and contrast religious histories, ideas, and practices.

Chapter 7 suggests something that most of us already know: we live in a very complex world, and religious forms have had to adapt themselves to that complexity by acknowledging many different ways of looking at religion. I offer a simplified version of that complexity by suggesting that three approaches to the religious world compete with one another for our mental time: the premodern, modern, and postmodern ways of looking at the world.

Chapter 8 identifies trajectories that the study of religion appears to be taking and then extrapolates those trajectories into the future. What challenges does the religion student of tomorrow face? What makes the discipline of religious studies so important today? Why does it matter?

If you have already done some study of religion, you may have a head start on the skills required, and you may have already run into the different mind-sets that different religious adherents bring to the respective faiths. It may even be clear to you how important the study of religion is in the world today, and you are ready to take on the challenge. If so, in the next three chapters you will see something different than what the brand-new student sees.

For example, when you read about the three fundamental skills in chapter 6, it may occur to you that beyond these three skills, serious research demands a tool kit of additional, specialized skills. If you are contemplating a quantitative research project based on the results of a large survey, for example, you will need to develop statistical expertise that you may or may not have acquired.

When reading chapter 7, you will already know that comprehending the features of premodern, modern, and postmodern religion is just the first step in understanding what is going on religiously in a specific culture. The next step is to discern how those three religious epistemologies not only relate to one another but are also expressed in this time and place.

Chapter 8 is an exercise in prognostication, really, and when it comes to predicting the future, everyone is an expert. You may have some important contributions to make to this prophetic exercise. What do you think is going to happen to the study of religion in the years to come, and how might you, with your unique skill set, contribute to that project? What can you offer because of who you are that no one else can contribute?

At the very least, when you finish reading the three chapters that make up part 3 you should be able to read religious texts with more discernment and with a better appreciation of what you need to work on to read them even better. You should also be able to collect data about living religions and active religious people, projecting ways to improve that process. Finally, you should begin to master the ways in which you analyze the data you collect. By seeing what is important and what is peripheral, you can discern the sense of the whole from what William James calls the "wild facts" that clamor for our attention but, on closer examination, turn out to be unimportant exceptions to the rule.

You should be able to devise a research plan, not just for your subject matter but also for yourself. Is religion really something you want to study? If so, what special gifts do you bring to the table? What kind of a developmental plan can you devise that will answer the question *Why and how should I study religion?*

6

The Scholarly Skills

Studying Texts, Collecting Ethnographic Data, Comparing and Contrasting Ideas

As we saw in chapter 2, students of religion need to equip themselves with at least three basic research skills: the linguistic ability to study texts, the anthropologist's ethnographic research methodology, and the philosopher's facility in handling concepts. That is, scholars of religion must be able to work with texts, people, and ideas. These are the *primary skills* with which every student of religion should have some facility—equivalent to the carpenter's measure, saw, and hammer or the fisherman's bait, cast, and troll.

It is likely that you will gravitate toward one or another of these skills. This is to be expected. It is certainly true of the great scholars of religion. Philosophers of religion, such as Ninian Smart,[1] incline toward handling concepts; linguists of religion, such as Wendy

---

1. Ninian Smart (1927–2001) was a British religious studies scholar who specialized in communicating the importance of his craft to secular audiences. Among his many books and contributions was his well-known division of religion into seven dimensions: ritual, narrative, experiential, institutional, ethical, doctrinal, and material.

Doniger O'Flaherty,[2] are predisposed to the study, communication, and translation of texts; and anthropologists and sociologists of religion, such as Robert Priest,[3] focus their research efforts on ethnography—collecting data in the field, doing survey research, and interviewing. These might be called the *preferred skills* of particular scholars and students. Yet the doctoral programs in religious studies all recognize the need for the development of all three skills in order to do research in the field and to be able to teach these skills to future students.

As research of a specific sort gets more refined, a set of what might be called *specialist skills* needs to be developed. Data collected by anthropologists through their use of ethnographic method, for example, can be designated for use in either qualitative or quantitative studies. Indeed, the use of quantifiable data requires a deep understanding of statistics. Philosophers may be interested in understanding the religious concepts they study in terms of their logic and coherence, their "eliteness" versus their popularity, and/or their apparent ethical value. Linguists, in addition to the pure comprehension and translation of texts, are also interested in the history, authorship, editorial development, authority, and availability of the texts under consideration. Each of these specialist skills requires training in order for students to become masters in their use.

Students of religion learn their skills in different ways, combining basic education, apprenticeships, and research experimentation. All graduate studies programs in religion require a one- or two-semester course in basic research methods. Just as we learned in grade school to count, spell, read, and write, undergraduate and graduate students in religion are taught to survey, interview, exegete, translate, observe, and analyze. Most of the time the basic course in research methods is taught as a survey, covering all the basic methods of research in

2. Wendy Doniger O'Flaherty (b. 1940) teaches at the University of Chicago. She is an Indologist and Sanskrit scholar who is clear about her scholarship, describing herself as one inclined to studying texts. Among her many publications is a translation of 108 chapters of the Rig Veda.

3. Robert Priest, professor of mission and anthropology at Trinity Evangelical Divinity School, has been a pioneer in showing Christian missiologists and theologians how to use the findings of anthropology in their work. His work usefully relates ethnography to the study of religion.

religious studies, even if students are expected in other parts of their program (such as researching and writing a dissertation) to focus solely on one or two research methodologies.[4]

The learning of scholarly skills, however, does not end when one passes a single course in religion, satisfies the requirements for a major in religious studies, or even receives a PhD in a field of religious studies. Apprenticeships of one sort or another continue the refining of scholarly skills after the basic courses and programs of study are over. Postdoctoral programs, the formal mentoring of a senior colleague, or the informal mentoring that comes from guild participation (where interactions with senior colleagues are common and expected) all play an important role in the development of religious studies scholarship. Even in such collaborative efforts as coauthoring essays and books, one's collaborative partners continue the refining of research techniques in reciprocal fashion. Scholars of religion learn from one another.

To be sure, research refinements continue simply as a function of doing research. Even the solitary researcher continues to learn from projects as he or she pursues additional projects. Similar growth in research proficiency takes place in the classroom, where the process of teaching the standard research methods to students invariably adds to one's own store of research capacity and sophistication.[5] In the case of senior scholars, new ways of doing things may emerge after years of doing research in a particular subdiscipline of religious studies—ways that become research breakthroughs in their own right.

A word about guild participation: it is essential that the budding scholar of religion begin participating in a scholarly guild as soon as possible. That is, as soon as a student has decided on a research paper topic in his or her introductory course or (for those further along in their studies) a dissertation topic and its accompanying research

4. The following three texts are good introductions to research methodologies: Mortimer Adler, *How to Read a Book* (New York: Touchstone, 1972); Robert Emerson, Rachel Fretz, and Linda Shaw, *Writing Ethnographic Fieldnotes* (Chicago: University of Chicago Press, 1995); Terry C. Muck, *The Mysterious Beyond: A Basic Guide to Studying Religion* (Grand Rapids: Baker, 1993).

5. When I take a close look at the origin of the ideas I chose to pursue in my religious studies career, they have generally come from one of two sources: class discussions with students and the most astute researcher I know, my wife, Frances Adeney.

methodology, he or she should join and attend the annual meetings of the guild in which scholars are doing similar research and using the same methodologies. Yet even before that choice is made, students interested in religion should consider attending at least one meeting of the American Academy of Religion.[6] Depending on one's research field, it is also important to join the Society of Biblical Literature, the Society of Christian Ethics, the Society for the Scientific Study of Religion, the International Historians of Religion and/or the religion division of the American Anthropological Association. In addition, one should subscribe to the appropriate journals published by each of these guild groups.

Participation in an appropriate guild or guilds is essential for progress in the development of one's interest in the study of religion. Just as someone interested in becoming a pastor should first be interested in attending church, so someone interested in studying religion should first attend an American Academy of Religion meeting to see what the community life is all about. Associations with colleagues made at guild meetings will last a lifetime. Some of these associations will turn into deep friendships, though the occasional animosity may also surface. One word of caution: though one's scholarly guild and the relationships developed therein can seem to be more important than relationships with faculty colleagues back home, faculty relationships are also crucial. Put another way, guild and faculty relationships are equally important, if different in the form and functions they take.[7]

Clearly there is much more than meets the eye in a religious studies scholar's skill set development. Entire books are written on each of the methods mentioned above. In this chapter, however, I limit the discussion to the three basic skills of engaging texts, engaging people, and engaging ideas. This is based on the conviction that these

6. I attended my first meeting of the American Academy of Religion in Chicago in 1974. I heard a presentation by the great Chicago scholar of religion, Mircea Eliade, and I was hooked on religious studies for life.

7. One lives with faculty colleagues on a day-to-day basis; guild colleagues are met once or twice a year. Although not a hard and fast rule, I found that guild colleagues tend to be inspiriting and generative of new ideas or new ways of looking at things, while faculty colleagues (who tend to know me better) help me to make necessary adjustments to projects already in process.

three skills are universal to all religion scholars—a kind of ABCs of religious studies. One must learn them before more detailed methods are engaged, in the same way that a basic understanding of arithmetic must be mastered before moving on to algebra and calculus. That being the case, let's take a look, in turn, at studying texts, collecting ethnographic data, and comparing and contrasting ideas.

Studying Texts

It is difficult to imagine doing religious studies without the ability to study texts in some form. For example, many religions define themselves by their authoritative literature—their "bibles." In order to understand the religion it is necessary to understand these defining texts. For some scholars of religion, studying defining texts and the commentarial and secondary literature that surround the fundamental texts is the sum total of being a scholar of a particular religion. For these scholars, studying texts is not just a primary skill of religious studies; it is also their preferred skill, which encompasses a range of specialist skills that are primarily linguistic in nature.

Those of us who come from such "traditions of the book" often forget that many religions do not have authoritative texts. Rather than written texts, some religions have only oral teachings and stories. Being a student of one of these religious traditions means making discovery through archaeological remains and direct observation of religious behaviors. Typically, it also means that these scholars learn from what others have written about those religions, which brings us back to studying texts. Though these texts are not primary sources or authoritative texts, they make up an important body of work about a religion—the so-called secondary sources.

The first step a scholar of religion takes in planning his or her study of a religious tradition is determining which written sources, both primary and secondary, are available and then developing a reading and study plan for mastering that religion's normative literature. There is no skipping this step. Until the normative literature is identified and the process of mastery is begun, a scholar is no different from a dilettante or dabbler. Once the normative literature is identified, however, scholarship can begin.[8]

Mastering the normative literature of a religion—authoritative texts, commentarial literature, and secondary literature—cannot be simply summarized under the heading of "reading." The act of reading must be unpacked to include at least five subcategories of what reading in a certain religious tradition entails: reading for comprehension, studying backgrounds, learning the language, translating texts, and making applications. When the act of reading is unpacked in this way, the student turns from the reading of texts to the studying of texts—and by these acts becomes a scholar.

Reading for Comprehension

Scholars of religion don't read texts for enjoyment. That is not to say they don't enjoy what they read. Most do. But scholarly reading places the focus on another goal: understanding what religious texts mean to the author, to the author's original audience, and to readers today. To understand what they read, scholars need to develop and apply critical thinking skills to the material at hand. This sort of reading for comprehension is the baseline skill of all religious studies. If you cannot read well and read fairly quickly, you cannot be a religious studies scholar.

Studying Backgrounds

A great aid to reading well is knowing how to research the history of a text even before critical thinking skills are applied to the content. Is the author of the text known? If known, what is the author like? If unknown, why is the text anonymous? Is the material original to the author, or is the author more of an editor who has compiled existing work? What principles have guided whatever changes have occurred in the work over the years? How available is the text and its interpretation to different classes of people within the community of adherents? What role does this text play to the members of the

---

8. I can't resist one further comment about this step. Do not be discouraged by the time it takes to develop an authoritative bibliography for a project. A good book is hard to find. In some ways it is like the foundation of a building: a bad foundation means a rickety building, just as a bad bibliography makes for mediocre research.

religious community who embrace it? What level of authority does the text have for adherents? Is that authority growing or declining?

Learning the Language

If the text is in your native language, great. If not, you must learn the language in which it is written. Preferably, you must be able to read the language, speak it, and write in it. This skill is nonnegotiable.[9] To be sure, there are scholars who do not learn the primary language(s) of the religions they study. They are the poorer for it, and they will never achieve the level of proficiency in their scholarship that they desire and that the scholarly community needs. Learn the language. Learn the language. Learn the language.

Translating Texts

However, it is optional as to whether you put the language to use by translating religious texts into other languages. Although making translations of religious texts is enormously important and must be done by someone, not every scholar needs to translate. Translation is more than a mechanical exercise; it is closer to an art. It makes use of personal, intellectual, and emotional gifts that not everyone has available to them. While it is desirable to have multiple translations of important texts, the number needed is not infinite. A few really good translations are more important than many average ones.

Making Applications

Once comprehension is mastered, the scholar of religion is expected to make applications in order to tell others what the texts mean to us

9. While English may be the lingua franca of the world, particularly the scientific world, "foreign" languages are still key in the social sciences and humanities. The religions you study will determine which foreign languages are important to know. Typically, you will need three types of languages: (1) a world language—one of the ten languages with over 100 million speakers (Mandarin, English, Hindi, Spanish, Russian, Arabic, Bengali, Portuguese, Indonesian, and French); (2) an ecclesial language—the language of religious texts, such as Latin, Sanskrit, Greek, Hebrew, etc.; and (3) a scholarship language—the languages of secondary scholarship, i.e., German, French, Italian, Russian, etc.

today. This service must not be done too quickly; conclusions about texts and their applications must be made slowly and modestly. A good scholar is cautious and reserved about what a text means—what its author intended, what its original hearers heard, and what it means for readers today.

Much more could be said about the importance of reading and studying religious texts. As a scholarly skill, its importance cannot be overemphasized. Without it scholarship fails. When reading and studying are done well and with respect for the subject matter, other doors of discovery open.

Collecting Ethnographic Data

Two of the most impressive collectors of ethnographic data in the emerging discipline of anthropology in the twentieth century were Clifford Geertz and Margaret Mead. Both were field researchers and spent several years studying unstudied people groups and tribes; Geertz worked in Indonesia and Morocco, and Mead lived among the Samoan Indians in Papua New Guinea. Among this "second wave" of anthropologists, several years of fieldwork became standard practice, which was a vast improvement over so-called armchair anthropolo-gists who sat in their comfortable offices in the West, organizing and theorizing other peoples' observations. The new breed made their own observations, such as Franz Boas among the Baffin Island Inuit, Bronislaw Malinowski among the Trobriand Islanders, A. R. Radcliffe among various Australian tribes, and Paul Radin among Native American tribes. Two or three years of field research, especially among a previously unstudied people group, became the ideal and model that all aspiring anthropologists emulated.

The method used to study these people groups is called *ethnogra-phy*—the systematic study of peoples and cultures, using observation techniques that attempt to discern the point of view of the peoples being observed. For an anthropologist studying a people group, the result of fieldwork is multiple notebooks filled with observations that include: individual and communal behavior (religion being one part of that overall behavior); studies of how people are related to one another (kinship); and the people group's place in its current environment, both the physical world and other humans (i.e., its relationship with other tribes). Ethnography is such a powerful research tool that ethnographic-type studies are not done strictly by anthropologists or of isolated tribal groups. Painstaking attention to behavior can also be applied to any individual or group of people in any physical and geographical setting. In addition to anthropologists and sociologists, psychologists and even biologists use ethnographic techniques of research.

Geertz (1926–2006) was an American anthropologist who studied at Harvard under Talcott Parsons and taught at the University of Chicago and Princeton University. His field research for his doctorate and his first published work was done in Indonesia, where he became especially interested in Islam. Geertz published many essays from that ethnographic research, including a famous anthropological observation of Balinese cockfighting. His Indonesian research also produced three books, including *The Religion of Java*.[10] That interest led to his second venue of field research in North Africa, particularly Morocco, and resulted in his important work, *Islam Observed*.[11]

Geertz's research in Morocco produced one of his most important insights, especially for religious studies students and scholars. In Morocco, a largely Muslim culture, Geertz expected to find the same Islam he had studied in some detail in Indonesia (*The Religion of Java*), which is also a largely Muslim culture. He found Islam all right, but it was a different Islam than the one he had encountered in Java. *Islam Observed* details these findings, which can be summarized for religion students in this way: even though you know the basic theoretical and theological teachings of a religious tradition, don't be surprised at the radically different manifestations of that religion in different cultures. In other words, don't assume you know until you observe.

Of course, collecting data with the goal of understanding that data from the point of view of the subjects being studied raises all

10. Clifford Geertz, *The Religion of Java* (Chicago: University of Chicago Press, 1960).

11. Clifford Geertz, *Islam Observed: Religious Development in Morocco and Indonesia* (Chicago: University of Chicago Press, 1968).

the questions about objectivity that I addressed in chapter 2, using Joachim Wach's observations. As much as anthropological ethnographers attempt to remove themselves from the observational dynamics of fieldwork, they are still there. Their presence makes a difference in the observations and must be accounted for in the applications, implications, and conclusions of the study. There is no pure ethnography, only ethnography that attempts to account for the influence of the observer in the interpretation of the data.

Margaret Mead (1901–78) was an American anthropologist, a student of Boas and Ruth Benedict at Columbia University. Mead became famous for a book that resulted from her rigorous ethnographic study in Samoa. In *Coming of Age in Samoa*, Mead relates the results of her observations of Samoan children and the development of their sexual mores as they go through the process of becoming adults.[12] Her conclusions are still controversial, but the larger contribution of her work to anthropology, and indirectly to the anthropology of religion, is more important. In *Coming of Age in Samoa*, the larger point is that the Samoans raise their children differently than Americans do, especially when it comes to their understanding of sexual mores. Boas summarizes this implication roughly this way: while courtesy, modesty, good manners, and ethical conformity seem to be universal across cultures, the specifics of what makes for courtesy, modesty, good manners, and ethical conformity in each culture are not; they can be radically different from culture to culture.

The implications of this insight for the study of religion in various cultures are important. While transcendence, lack, release, and reconciliation may be almost universal across religious traditions, the specifics of each are radically different from religion to religion and, within religions, from culture to culture, as Geertz's experiences with Islam in Indonesia and Morocco show.

An enjoyable way to access the flavor of Mead and her work in Samoa is to read *Euphoria*, a novel based on her life and her relationships with two of her three husbands, written by Lily King.[13]

---

12. Margaret Mead, *Coming of Age in Samoa* (New York: Mentor, 1928).
13. Lily King, *Euphoria* (New York: Grove, 2015).

Comparing and Contrasting Ideas

Once appropriate texts have been identified and read and field data has been collected, the ideas that emerge need to be understood, analyzed, and applied. This is where basic philosophical skills come to the fore. Especially important—particularly within a field once called comparative religion—is the facility to compare and contrast ideas from two or more different religions. In this formulation, *compare* means to find similarities between related phenomena, and *contrast* means to identify the differences between and among the phenomena. The common expectation of such a literary and intellectual exercise is that whenever two related items from different religions are compared and contrasted, one will find a balance between similarities and differences—even though that is not always the case.[14]

The process of comparing and contrasting can be roughly laid out in a six-step process:

1. State the comparison in a single sentence. (To demonstrate this process, we are going to compare the Christian conception of salvation with the Hindu notion of release.)

2. In a short paragraph, give a definition of Christian salvation; in a second paragraph, give a definition of Hindu release.

3. Rehearse the brief history of the development of each concept in each religion. Make clear whether your comparison is done based on current understandings or focused on a specified historical era.

4. Discuss the role that each concept plays in its respective religion, noting especially how central (or peripheral) each is in the overall religious conceptualization and practice.

14. It may be that we are all predisposed to overemphasize either similarities or differences. And it may be true that one's disposition in this matter is the surest tip-off to one's ideological biases. Even so, this does not vitiate the value of doing compare and contrast exercises. Acknowledging these biases should not lead to an unscholarly bias, i.e., insisting on an exact balance between similarities and differences. The data must speak for itself; some comparisons will lead to more similarities than differences and vice versa.

5. The comparison proper: identify similarities discovered in the above process and list the differences between them that became clear.

6. Conclude with a summary statement of the compare and contrast exercise.

A formal comparison covers all six steps. Many comparisons, however, are done in an abbreviated, more informal way. Both types of comparing and contrasting can be valuable. In each, it is important to be clear about the reason why the comparison is being done in the first place. In general, comparisons can be done in order to seek the falseness of each comparator, to seek which of the two comparators is better, to satisfy the researcher's curiosity (whether spiritual or otherwise), or to discover truth—by which I mean the clearest statement of each that can be made, especially in regard to their relationship to each other. For religious studies, the last is the correct motivation and goal.

The German scholar Rudolf Otto provides a classic example of a full-fledged comparison of this sort. Otto was a historian of religion, best known for his book *The Idea of the Holy.*[15] But his comparison is titled *India's Religion of Grace and Christianity Compared and Contrasted.*[16] The book, a classic example of comparison, should be read by all students of religion in order to see what interreligious comparison of ideas is like.

Otto begins by stating his comparison early on. He wants to compare and contrast the doctrine of grace in both Indian religion and Christianity. In the opening chapters of this short work (only 110 pages) he clearly defines what grace means in Christianity and what grace means in Hinduism, especially in the *bhakti* tradition of Hinduism. Through these early definitions, Otto reveals several things. While he is extraordinarily knowledgeable of both traditions, he also has a good sense of how compatible and similar the two doctrines are, which serves the purpose of showing how important this compare

15. Rudolf Otto, *The Idea of the Holy,* trans. John W. Harvey (1917; repr., New York: Oxford University Press, 1958).

16. Rudolf Otto, *India's Religion of Grace and Christianity Compared and Contrasted* (New York: Macmillan, 1930).

SIMILARITIES AND DIFFERENCES

Religions, including Christianity, can be considered in terms of beliefs or teachings, basic values or ethical ideals, rituals or practices, and institutions. When Christianity is compared with other religions such as Hinduism, Buddhism, Islam, Shintoism, Sikhism, and Daoism, it becomes clear that there are similarities to aspects of some religions as well as differences. Each religious tradition needs to be considered on its own in relation to Christianity, and both similarities and differences need to be acknowledged. Think of a continuum with strong similarities on one end and strong differences on the other.

Similarities			Differences
Teachings	Values	Rituals	Institutions

A religion such as Islam will have greater similarities to Christianity in teachings than, for example, Buddhism, although Buddhism will have similarities to Christianity in values and ethical ideals.

From Terry Muck, Harold Netland, and Gerald McDermott, eds., *Handbook of Religion* (Grand Rapids: Baker Academic, 2014), 25.

and contrast exercise is. One comes away from a reading of these initial chapters believing that "grace" is present in both traditions.

After establishing this initial similarity, Otto begins to complexify the comparison, which is not as simple as it seems. For example, one tradition of Hinduism especially, the *bhakti* tradition, gives the most attention to grace while another very strong tradition, Vedanta, does not give as much. By identifying two outstanding Hindu teachers—Ramanuja and Sankara—as representatives of the two traditions, Otto not only compares the *bhakti* and Vedanta traditions but also outlines the Christian teaching on grace and its development in Christian history.

In chapter 4 of *India's Religion of Grace*, Otto then begins what might be called the comparison proper, in which he continues to acknowledge the similarities between Hindu grace and Christian grace while also noting, in some detail, the differences between the two. These differences culminate in what Otto sees as the primary and essential contrast between the two traditions when it comes to grace, that is, the different roles that grace plays in each tradition. He argues that in

Christianity grace is essential and central, the axis on which the religion turns, while in Indian religion grace is important but not central—and certainly not the axis on which the whole religious edifice turns.

Otto comes to an intriguing conclusion. (Remember that in any compare and contrast exercise, one normally looks for a balance between the two elements. State what is similar but also what is different.) It may be, Otto argues, that Christians have been too eager to privilege their religion's doctrine of grace in an attempt to show that it is not only the defining characteristic of Christian teaching but is also unique to Christianity. In other words, Christians tend to stress the contrast side of the compare and contrast exercise. Otto argues for more balance in Christian understanding by showing that grace is part and parcel of Indian religion; he emphasizes the similarities, the comparison part of the exercise.

On the Indian side, Otto continues, the opposite has been true. Indian teachers perhaps overemphasize the similarities between their understanding of grace and that of the Christian understanding. This may be to some extent because of the Christian mission insistence on the uniqueness of Christianity, but it also seems to reveal an essential Hindu trait of inclusiveness and wholeness. Regardless, Otto makes the point that Indian thinkers might be well served to more carefully acknowledge the contrast side of the compare-contrast exercise in order to show the important and essential differences between the two teachings on grace.

Conclusion

As I mentioned at the beginning of this chapter, much more can be said on each of these three study skills. There is no shortage of material on how to read texts better, how to do ethnography, and how to compare and contrast the ideas that emerge when a student begins to study religion. But I would like to offer just a few words on how the beginning student can further his or her facility in each of these three skills.

The essential way to become a better reader is to read—a lot. The more a student immerses him- or herself in the texts the better. Since the study of religion involves so much reading, students might even consider taking a speed-reading course, particularly one that emphasizes both speed and comprehension. I would also recommend reading Mortimer Adler's *How to Read a Book*,[17] particularly if one needs to recapture the joy of reading (if it has been somehow lost—or never experienced in the first place). Make no mistake, reading should be a joy, not an obligation and burden.

Similarly, the essential way to become a better ethnographer is to do ethnography. Perhaps begin by recognizing that more than meets the eye in your everyday life is, in essence, ethnography. An initial curiosity about other people and what makes them tick, followed in turn by talking with and reading about them, is ethnography in its most popular form. Needless to say, read a book on ethnography—there are many.[18] Some of the most helpful books are written for disciplines outside the boundaries of religious studies. Three of my favorites come from sociology (*Diffusion of Innovations*), management theory (*Organizational Culture and Leadership*), and leadership studies (*The Innovator's Dilemma*).[19] Common to all is the strong suggestion that the deepest learning comes from face-to-face interactions with the subjects of one's study, which is what ethnography is all about.

Finally, hone your compare and contrast skills by continuing to develop your capacity for critical thinking. I strongly recommend you join the Foundation for Critical Thinking.[20] Read some of their short books on the various elements of critical thought. Consider attending one of their conferences. Force yourself to participate in the question and answer time after lectures. Make sure the questions you ask are to the point and clear. Evaluate your own writing and thinking by comparing what you do with critical thinking theory.

Don't think that these skills will mature overnight. Becoming better at all three takes years of practice and should be seen as a lifetime learning goal rather than a task that can be quickly mastered.

17. Adler, *How to Read a Book*.

18. One of the best new examples, written especially for those interested in the relationship of fieldwork to Christian theology, is Christian Scharen, *Fieldwork in Theology* (Grand Rapids: Baker Academic, 2015).

19. Everett Rogers, *Diffusion of Innovations* (New York: Free Press, 1962); Edgar Schein, *Organizational Culture and Leadership* (San Francisco: Jossey-Bass, 2010); and Clayton Christensen, *The Innovator's Dilemma* (New York: HarperBusiness, 2000).

20. See www.criticalthinking.org for more information.

Why I Study Religion

MICHAEL BARKUN, SYRACUSE UNIVERSITY

My entry into the study of religion nearly half a century ago was abrupt and completely unexpected. At the time, I was a graduate student in political science, and political science in those days—the early 1960s—ignored religion almost entirely. The dominant view held that societies around the world were secularizing and that religion was destined to be a politically marginal factor. That view would change, of course, by the late 1970s with the emergence of militant Islam and the New Christian Right, but in the 1960s it was unquestioned.

I was at work on a dissertation about international law, and one day, seeking escape, I wandered around the paperback section of a Chicago bookstore seeking something that had nothing to do with my research. A dramatic book cover caught my eye; it was filled with billowing black clouds, set against a white background. I picked the book up and examined it. The subtitle spoke of "revolutionary messianism" in the Middle Ages, as well as the Reformation and its connection with totalitarianism. This arresting thesis is advanced by Norman Cohn, whose seminal work, *The Pursuit of the Millennium*, I held in my hand.

At the time, I knew nothing about either revolutionary messianism or the millennium and knew no more about the Middle Ages or the Reformation than I remembered from my undergraduate Western Civilization course. But the idea that ancient and obscure religious groups lay at the root of modern totalitarianism piqued my interest. I bought the book. Like many of its readers, I was swept away not only by Cohn's prose but also by the audacity of his thesis (which, by the way, I continue to believe is fundamentally correct). As time permitted, I began to dip into other works on millennialism, not only in religious studies but also in sociology of religion, anthropology, and other disciplines.

A year or two later I took up a faculty position. My dissertation needed to be turned into a book, and I had taken on some other obligations connected with my original work on international law. Like most junior faculty, I was preoccupied with the quest for tenure. But I resolved early on that my true research direction needed to be millennialism and that my other commitments had to be wrapped up as quickly as possible so that I would be free to pursue it. I was able to secure a research leave in 1970 that allowed me to read deeply in millenarian studies, leading me not only to the many European sects described by Cohn but also to Melanesian cargo cults, Native American Ghost Dancers, and the Taiping rebels in China. Four books on millennialism and abundant papers, articles, and book chapters followed over the years.

I began with the problem of the causes of millenarian movements, which I examine in *Disaster and the Millennium* (1974). That was followed by an investigation of the surge in millenarianism in my own area of the country, upstate New York; in *Crucible of the Millennium* (1986) I explore the so-called Burned-Over District of the 1840s. After this long immersion in nineteenth-century chiliasm, I was anxious to find some unexamined twentieth-century case to research next. I found one among the white supremacist believers in Christian Identity. A search for its origins provided the basis for *Religion and the Racist Right* (1993, rev. ed. 1997). Dealing with the worldview of white supremacists was unpleasant, but it also provided an opportunity to study religion built around visions of conspiracy. That led me to look more broadly at the intersection of religion and conspiracy in *A Culture of Conspiracy* (2003, rev. ed. 2013).

The chance encounter with Cohn's book almost fifty years ago was life-changing for me, and I have often thought that had it been shelved spine out rather than cover out, my scholarly life would have been far different and far less interesting.

7

Perspectival Objectivity

From Premodern to Modern to Postmodern

Four years ago, as I was leaving my teaching post in theological education, someone asked me whether things had changed in seminary teaching during my quarter century of classroom work, and if so, how. I gave the question quite a bit of thought. I realized that several things had changed dramatically in my pedagogical career: We moved from snail mail to email to Facebook. From blackboards to overheads to internet. From lecture halls to discussion groups to dialogues in the field. From denominations to national churches to global religion. From hardcover to paperback to Kindle. From hardcopies to tapes to discs to thumb drives to "the cloud." From typewriters to computers, carbon copies to photocopies. From real to virtual. But the biggest change—the one I wanted to talk about—was the change in students.

"How have students changed?" I was asked.

"Many ways, I suppose," I answered. "But perhaps the most important way is how they think."

I went on to explain that answer briefly. It was, after all, an interview, not a book chapter. So I will summarize what I told the interviewer, but since this *is* a book chapter, I would like to unpack my answer more fully and relate it specifically to religious studies. Here is the brief version of what I said in the interview.

> When I first started teaching theology I saw my goal as facilitating students as they moved from the naive, largely unreflected-on faith with which they entered seminary to a conscious, systematic expression of doctrine. Although I was in a Presbyterian seminary and then a Wesleyan one, I was not as concerned with what systematic tradition the students chose to engage, just that they were able to express a consistent, coherent theological tradition that they could embrace wholly and utilize fully in their private, ecclesial, and public lives as vocational theologians.
>
> I believe that my earliest students joined me in this endeavor. They worked not only to understand and incorporate Calvin or Wesley as the traditions had been passed on to them but also to put their own stamp on things, being aware of the boundaries of the Reformed and Wesleyan traditions. To be sure, they would sometimes strain against the boundaries. My job, as I saw it then, was to help them recognize when they were straining and why, as well as the pros and cons of stretching the restraining ropes. All the while, they were developing a consistent, coherent theological stance.
>
> Somewhere along the way that began to change. Students continued to be interested in theology but not so much in the "consistent, coherent" part. More precisely, over the years they seemed less and less convinced that one's theology needed to be consistent and coherent. What theology really needed was to be "balanced" and "realistic" and "useful" in addressing the needs of a needy world. And if the standard of "balanced" and "realistic" and "useful" was met at a sacrifice of some "consistency and coherence," so be it. Time is short, and people are suffering; since theological traditions are, after all, human constructs, a certain lack of precision is acceptable, even laudable.
>
> The interesting thing about these changes in students is that it did not bother me, their teacher, very much. That may be because, as one of my theological colleagues put it ever so delicately, there are a lot of weeds in my theological garden. But perhaps I was being influenced and changed by the same societal dynamics confronting my students. I began to wonder just what those societal dynamics were and where we are, relative to the changes today.

Why begin this chapter with that memory? Because I would like to make the case that the same changes that so dramatically influenced my students over the course of thirty years of theological education are affecting not only the discipline of religious studies but also the student-scholars who study religion. I think the changes—call them changes in epistemology—that I observed in my students and described briefly above are real and ongoing, part of the zeitgeist of American society. I think those same dynamics are changing religious studies. And I think it behooves us to pay attention to them so that we can shape our scholarly endeavors in the study of religion to be faithful to our calling as religious studies scholars.

My argument is structured historically. A very common, shorthand way of talking about shifts in the zeitgeist (that is, the cultural influences that shape the way we look at the world) of the West is to divide human history into three eras: the premodern, the modern, and the postmodern. It is hard to argue with such a periodization, since it is so general and covers such large blocks of time. What is difficult about this division, however, is how to define the premodern, modern, and postmodern—how to relate those periodic changes in epistemology (i.e., ways of viewing the world) to religion specifically and then how to make a clear statement about where we stand now in relation to the premodern, modern, and postmodern ways of being religious in evidence today.

I just introduced a technical word in the last couple of paragraphs: *epistemology*. *Epistemology* is a philosophical term that refers to the study of the way we know things about the world in which we live. Philosophers, especially, spend quite a bit of time exploring the different ways people and cultures throughout the world organize and analyze the hundreds of sensations with which they are bombarded minute by minute—that is, the way they view and interpret the world. I believe that the changes I observed in my students over the years were epistemological at heart. And I believe I taught during a period of especially rapid and consequential change, from a modern epistemology to a postmodern epistemology. That shift is ongoing.

Premoderns understood the world in one way, and moderns understood it in another; in turn, postmoderns understand the world in a different way yet. Let's look at these three in more detail.

DOING A RELIGIOUS AUDIT

A religious audit is a systematic way of first discerning and then describing how religion is expressed in a particular culture at a particular time and place. The first step in doing a religious audit of a particular time and place is to answer the following questions:

1. What is the religious history of this place, with particular focus on the "original," indigenous religion?
2. What is the present-day, dominant world religion, and how did it come to dominate?
3. What new religious movements are present in this society? How prevalent are they? How many are there? Which are the strongest and most influential?
4. How do indigenous religious values still express themselves? Are the influences implicit or explicit?
5. Do the relationships between the dominant world religion and the new religious movements tend toward conflict, peaceful coexistence, or cooperation?

Use the following types of books:

1. A history of religion in this place. For example, James Huntley Grayson, *Korea: A Religious History* (New York: Routledge, 2002).
2. A history of the coming of the dominant world religion to this country, area, and culture. For example, Ian Charles Harris, *Cambodian Buddhism: History and Practice* (Honolulu: University of Hawaii Press, 2008).
3. The story of new religious movements in this country, area, and culture. For example, Helen Hardacre, *Kurozumikyō and the New Religions of Japan* (Princeton: Princeton University Press, 1986).
4. The continuing influence of indigenous religions. For example, Jack Weatherford, *Native Roots: How the Indians Enriched America* (New York: Ballantine Books, 1992).

As an example, for a religious audit of religion in Morocco, read the following books and use them to answer the five questions above:

Geertz, Clifford. *Islam Observed: Religious Development in Morocco and Indonesia*. Chicago: University of Chicago Press, 1968.

McMurray, David. *In and Out of Morocco: Smuggling and Migration in a Frontier Boomtown*. Minneapolis: University of Minnesota Press, 2001.

Terasse, Henri. *History of Morocco*. Casablanca: Atlantides, 1952.

Zeghal, Malika. *Islamism in Morocco: Religion, Authoritarianism, and Electoral Politics*. Princeton: Markus Wiener, 2008.

From Terry Muck, Harold Netland, and Gerald McDermott, eds., *Handbook of Religion* (Grand Rapids: Baker Academic, 2014), 5.

Premodern

What does *premodern* mean? In chapter 3 I explained what *premodern* means when it comes to religions of the premodern era. Robert Bellah's archaic and primitive religions are characterized by tribal structures and undifferentiated personal responsibilities and roles—that is, the religious, economic, cultural, social, and political arenas all tend to roll together, including the leadership roles. Like a ship at sea or an airplane in flight, the passengers are a single unit, isolated to a large degree from the rest of the world and kept in the charge of a "captain" who makes all the decisions (such as performing weddings, when required). Premoderns have faith in a god or gods, are committed to a single communal tradition, and usually hold as their highest good the harmony of the tribe.

But what does *premodern* mean when it comes to epistemology, that is, when it comes to the way in which members of premodern tribes look at and interpret the world? At minimum, we would do well not to underestimate the intelligence of premoderns or their ability to adapt to challenging conditions when required to do so. Claude Levi-Strauss, a French anthropologist and ethnographer who is sometimes called the "father of modern anthropology," wrote a classic book to that effect, *The Savage Mind*. In it, he argues that primitive peoples were every bit as intelligent as modern and postmodern ones; they simply went about their intellectual and adaptive tasks differently.[1] The epistemology of the "savage mind" may have been different from the modern mind or the postmodern mind, but not less intelligent or adaptive.

They were different largely as a result of two factors. The first is their isolated tribal structure. Premoderns met few people unlike themselves, and those limited contacts led to fewer innovations in terms of new ideas for doing things. The other factor is their limited resources. Although we need to be careful not to assign all tribal groups to the distant past, the premodern outlook was dominant in a time before the scientific revolution.[2] Tribal groups missed out on

1. Claude Levi-Strauss, *The Savage Mind* (Chicago: University of Chicago Press, 1962).
2. The scientific revolution can be said to have started with Nicolaus Copernicus's book *On the Revolution of the Heavenly Spheres* (Amherst, NY: Prometheus Books,

the snowballing effects of scientific findings and the development of wider communication networks and technologies, such as printing presses and books; they did not have the tools to communicate innovations to wider and wider circles of peoples.

Levi-Strauss is famous for an analogy he paints in *The Savage Mind*, in which he contrasts premodern people to modern people as bricoleurs and engineers, respectively. *Bricoleur* is a French word that refers to do-it-yourself people who use whatever is at hand to solve problems and make repairs. Bricoleur is what we might call putterers or tinkerers who unsystematically solve problems as they arise, using whatever "tools" are at hand. Engineers, however, approach problems by clearly identifying the nature of the problem, relating it to other problems of the same sort, and devising solutions that may require the development of new and specific tools (which they sometimes must create) to address them. Engineers are not limited to the resources of a single tribe; they have at their disposal the entire scientific community and are limited only by the time needed to procure resources from whatever source might have them.[3]

Modern

One of the earliest religious studies "engineers" was James George Frazer, author of *The Golden Bough*, first published in 1890.[4] Frazer was a Scottish social anthropologist and is considered, along with Levi-Strauss and Franz Boas, to be one of the founding fathers of anthropology. His lifelong scholarly project was to catalog the phe-

1995) in 1543 and ended with Isaac Newton's *Principia* (Amherst, NY: Prometheus Books, 1995) in 1687.

3. If bricoleurs are premodern and engineers are modern, then (to continue Levi-Strauss's analogy) what personage or role characterizes the postmodern? I suggest something akin to the blogger, who writes short essays on the internet. The blogger is not limited in resources like the premodern; he or she has, in a sense, the whole world at his or her fingertips through the internet and social media. The challenge of innovation is not in new ideas but in choosing among possible solutions to problems. The defining characteristic of the postmodern blogger is that those choices are made by individual authority, by what that person chooses.

4. James George Frazer, *The Golden Bough* (1890; abr. ed., Mineola, NY: Dover, 2002).

nomenon of all the religions and religious people of the world. He did this by creating cross-religious categories of religious phenomenon and listing under each of those categories all the religious phenomenon from around the world that fell into that category. The project was immense. By the time of Frazer's death in 1941, the complete unabridged version of *The Golden Bough* was thirteen volumes. Today it is most often read in its one-volume, abridged version, which was put together in the 1920s by Frazer and his wife, Lady Frazer.

Frazer's project was modern because it attempted to go outside any single "tribal" group or tradition and was intended to be comprehensive of all human religious perspectives. A planned endeavor, Frazer used tools from a number of academic disciplines to collect and evaluate data. He also created a new tool, a categorization schema that attempted to find places for all religious practices from all times and all places. Although Frazer himself traveled very little during his anthropological career, he collected an immense amount of data from ancient histories and questionnaires sent to Christian missionaries around the world.[5]

The nature of Frazer's project is aligned with the modern way of looking at the world. Frazer believed that human religious thought progresses through three stages: the primitive or magical, religion proper, and science. Although that schema has not proven to be reliable or even useful to scholars today, it was the best example of Frazer's engineering mind-set and his enormous energy in attempting to create a system for understanding the world.[6]

These attempts at global theorizing and explanatory laws and theses are typical of the modern way of looking at the world. The modern view relies first and foremost on the use of the scientific method, which consists of hypothesis, experiment, conclusion, and new hypothesis.

5. Frazer is considered "old school" by modern anthropologists, for whom field work is essential. As evidence of his "ivory tower" approach being a great weakness, modern anthropologists point out the many inaccuracies in his work, particularly the generalizations made from them. Whether it is entirely fair to judge him on this basis (he worked in an era without jet planes and internet communications) is for others to decide. An equally interesting judgment of his work is made on the basis of his purported anti-Christian bias. See Timothy Larsen, *The Slain God: Anthropologists and Christian Faith* (Oxford: Oxford University Press, 2014).

6. See James George Frazer, *Man, God, Immortality* (New York: Macmillan, 1927).

Over against the communal focus of the premodern way of looking at the world, the modern view valorizes the individual and his or her capacity to learn, know, and create. The modern mind-set believes in the inevitability of progress and the superiority of "now" over "then." It is difficult to put a start or end date on the modern mind-set since its beginning significantly overlaps with the premodern and its ending is ongoing, transitioning into the postmodern way of thinking. If dates must be assigned, the modern period began around 1500, and the postmodern consciousness began to surface in 1950.

It is difficult to overestimate the impact of the modern, for it has changed the world for the better in almost every way—from lengthening the human lifespan to vastly improved health care to the education of a greater proportion of the world's population. In light of these contributions, it is legitimate to ask why a new way of looking at the world, the postmodern, is becoming increasingly common.

Postmodern

The postmodern mindset is skeptical, nonlinear, participatory, practical, and particular.[7] In essence, it is in basic opposition to the modern, which is optimistic, linear, hierarchical, theoretical, and universal. The postmodern is best understood as an opposition to modernity rather than a movement with a positive agenda of its own.

So what was so wrong with the modern way of looking at things, especially in light of its contributions to human flourishing? One could point out some of the unresolved issues facing the world, such as war, racism, environmental degradation, and so forth. But that would be to slip into the modernist way of looking at things, since most of us (in our modern mode) still believe that science and social science will eventually hit on the right formulas to solve these problems.

The postmodern mind-set is not just the flip side of the modern but an entirely new way to look at things. Gerardus van der Leeuw

7. Many reference the publication of Jean Francois Lyotard, *The Postmodern Condition: A Report on Knowledge* (Minneapolis: University of Minnesota Press, 1984) as the published herald of the postmodern way of looking at the world.

was a philosopher of religion, and although he would not have even known what the word postmodern refers to, many of the ways in which he deals with religion in his classic two-volume work, *Religion in Essence and Manifestation*, anticipate the themes my students and postmodernism in general have come to represent.[8] Van der Leeuw recognized religion's shortcomings and was a realist about the pros and cons of religion around the world. Although he was a dedicated Christian, he was not a fundamentalist when it came to assessing Christianity's place in the world.

Perhaps the single word that best describes van der Leeuw's incipient postmodern tendencies is *dynamic*. Van der Leeuw understood that all religions are constantly changing, evolving entities and that what one religion stood for at one point in time could change dramatically in a single generation and still be considered the same religion. He taught that religions have an essential core, but that essence can appear in myriad shapes and sizes. Religions have an essence capable of manifesting itself in an almost unlimited number of cultural forms.

No section of *Religion in Essence and Manifestation* captures this better than chapters 93 and 94 in volume 2: "The Dynamic of Religions: Syncretisms and Missions" and "The Dynamic of Religions: Revivals and Reformations."[9] In just a few pages, van der Leeuw discusses (1) what happens to different religions when they come in contact with one another (short answer: they change); (2) something he calls "transposition," the capacity religions have to continue using the same words to describe their teachings even though the content of those teachings may change dramatically; and (3) mission, the reality that all religions and religious people want to witness to others regarding their religious beliefs. Regarding this last item, van der Leeuw sees mission as a feature of human religiosity but acknowledges that the idea of mission changes dramatically from religion to religion. He sometimes calls this propensity "testimony" and sees it as something religious people do both inadvertently and intentionally.

8. Gerardus van der Leeuw, *Religion in Essence and Manifestation*, 2 vols., trans. J. E. Turner (1938; repr., New York: Harper & Row, 1963).
9. Ibid., 2:609–12.

The postmodern way of looking at the world eschews systematic thinking in favor of the pragmatic. It is opposed to metaphysical master narratives that attempt to describe everything in a single story. It valorizes fluidity, change, and contextualization. Although van der Leeuw still found a place for an essential core to different religions, many of today's postmoderns do not. In a way, the postmodern is like the internet itself, accessible by anyone, anywhere, at any starting point. The person doing the accessing determines the "essences" of the internet simply by how he or she uses it. And that individualistic usage becomes truth simply by the act of usage.

How Premodern, Modern, and Postmodern Relate to One Another

It would be wrong to suggest that students and scholars of religion these days are postmoderns because they are still taught to look at religion in the world from the modern stance of a social scientist. But it would also be wrong to suggest that they are not influenced by the postmodern critique of modernism. A better way of looking at the modern and the postmodern mind-sets is to see them both as alive and well in terms of the influence they have on cultures around the world, especially cultures in the West. It might be beneficial to throw the premodern into the mix as well. Once something achieves religious status in a culture, even a premodern viewpoint, it is never completely abandoned. It may be driven underground and thought to be excised—or to use van der Leeuw's term, it may be "transposed"—but its continuing influence on the culture in question can always be traced back to its source.

Thus, in attempting to describe the way we see the world of religion today, it might be most accurate to say that we are influenced in our epistemologies by all three ways of thinking—the premodern, modern, and postmodern. But before I make an argument for that assertion, it might be a good idea to suggest the other options open to us. If, as I have just suggested, we have in our culture and its history all three ways of looking at the religions in this part of the world— the premodern, modern, and postmodern—how do they combine? I propose four possibilities.

The Dismiss Option

It may be that the religion question is the wrong question altogether. The New Atheists[10] take this position, claiming that the age of religion is gone (or needs to be) and should be replaced by other questions and answers. Talking about premodern religion, modern religion, and postmodern religion in anything other than a historical sense is useless. And since religion and God (or the gods) as described by each religion are the ultimate metaphysical constructs, some postmodernists are not religious at all. Unsurprisingly, they prefer the option of dismissing religion entirely.

The Privilege Option

When faced with three choices, one choice can be deemed correct and the other two eliminated. Either the premodern, the modern, or the postmodern is privileged over the other two, similar to a political election in which several candidates are running for office but only one vote can be cast. The choice can be based on several factors, but in the end only one is chosen and privileged as correct. Of course, few of us today would choose the premodern way of thinking as the one, true way, but the intellectual battle between the modern and postmodern can be seen everywhere.

The Ranking Option

According to the ranking option, all three choices are considered valid and important, but one choice is deemed the most important. And the preference of one option determines to some degree the nature of the other two options. In Wesleyan Christian theological thought, for example, four hermeneutical principles are deemed authoritative (Scripture, tradition, reason, and experience), but for many Wesleyans one of the four—Scripture—is considered the most important and either trumps the other three or determines the agenda of the conversation.[11] In our de facto way of thinking, the modern

10. See the introduction to this book for a short discussion of the New Atheists.
11. This is called the Wesleyan quadrilateral. See Don Thorsen, *The Wesleyan Quadrilateral: Scripture, Tradition, Reason, & Experience as a Model of Evangelical Theology* (Lexington: Emeth, 2005).

usually plays this role, with the premodern and postmodern playing subsidiary roles.

The Contextualization Option

In this option, the premodern, modern, and postmodern ways of thinking are all considered important, but time, place, and context determine which one is most influential in any given situation. In some situations the premodern belief in evil spirits spurs us to avoid walking through a cemetery late at night; in other situations a twenty-first-century trained physician determines the course of treatment for an illness, trumping the herbal medicine shaman who has an office down the street; and in yet another situation, a postmodern critique of a scientist's recommendation that medication be used to treat depression influences our choice to instead reintroduce the possibility of a transcendent healing source. Much like a carpenter who chooses among a saw, a hammer, a screwdriver, a level, or a chisel, depending on the task at hand, the contextualizer chooses either the premodern, modern, or postmodern way of thinking depending on the circumstances. In such a schema, consistency is the hobgoblin of traditionalist minds.

I believe that the fourth option is the best one: our epistemological choices are made according to the context. The three religious options we call premodern, modern, and postmodern each have positive ways of looking at religion, and each is present in most societal settings today. Together they influence us in a dynamic epistemology that I call *perspectival objectivity*.

Perspectival Objectivity

As religious studies students or scholars we cannot help but look at religion in a certain way. We either choose or are trained (or both) to have a way of looking at religion that best achieves the goals of the discipline. That is, we are to make faithful observations and fashion them into defensible theories that others can use (e.g., policy makers) to make decisions about religious matters. We consciously choose to eschew the skeptical way of looking at religion, and we consciously give up the theological way of looking at world religion. While we make these choices in our roles as religious studies students/scholars, we have not totally abandoned the skeptical and the theological. Both are available to us in our other life roles. But as religious studies scholars we limit ourselves to what can be observed according to scientific principles. Still, we must choose between premodern science (what Levi-Strauss calls bricolage), modern science (the engineer mentality), and postmodern science (ruthlessly acknowledging both contextual factors and human limitations). How do we do that? Consider the following statement (my summary of perspectival objectivity):

> In demanding that we approach our tasks as students of religion with a posture of relative objectivity, we use one primary method of study (a scholarly tradition), which is augmented by other traditions as needed, confident and aware that what we discover, interpret, and communicate will advance our knowledge base of world religion, the primary goal of all religious studies.

Let's unpack that statement, which also serves as a definition of perspectival objectivity, by looking at three of its primary elements.

Relative Objectivity

We still attempt objectivity. It is still a goal, even if in the end we realize it is not achievable, at least as it has been understood in the past. For the perspectival objectivist, objectivity is important, but we cannot come close to achieving it as individual researchers; it must be approached in community. Objectivity takes a community of similarly devoted students of religion to assess one another's work, not just for mutual accountability to objectivity but to stimulate one another's work. The goal is still objectivity, but we need one another to seek it.

Tradition Based

We use our traditions and their specific epistemological tools, but we do not feel bound exclusively to them. We are willing to use other critical thinking tools when the subject matter and the context call for them. That is, one can be a historian of religion, a phenomenologist, a functionalist, or a structuralist in terms of critical thinking approach but still be open to the findings of other religious scholars, even using their methodologies when the subject matter calls for it. Religious studies is known for its use of multiple research methodologies.

Perspective Confidence

As a result of our realization that we cannot avoid having a specific perspective, a perspective that may or may not be the same as our colleague across the hall, we accept that we do not need to eschew or apologize for our perspective. All human knowledge is conditioned by context, and all human contexts are constantly changing. We need to be aware of the influence of context, and we need to acknowledge that changing contexts affect both method and results. That being said, we must start somewhere, and being based in a specific tradition of research (and belief) is unavoidable.

Conclusion

The way we think follows from the tools we have available to think with. The way we think changes when the tools we have change.

Premodern human beings had limited tools to use when faced with a thinking problem: they simply looked around and made use of tribal custom and communal decision making. There was little communication with those outside the tribe and certainly not an exchange of ideas. Over time, perhaps, innovations in thinking were made, but it was a slow and painstaking process of trial and error. The only standards against which to measure the advantage of new ways of thinking were limited to tribal sharing, and like all small groups, change came at a slow drip. In such a climate of innovation deprivation, it is no surprise that faith in God or the gods filled the vacuum of creative thinking.

Modern humans in the West changed dramatically when human creativity was given a boost by the Renaissance, the Reformation, and the Enlightenment. Faith in God no longer had to make up for the paucity of human reason. The incredible tool of the scientific method suddenly returned faith to its rightful place of relating to the gods, without asking the gods to double as innovators and inventors. Science provided a means of cross-cultural communication, and the sharing of innovation became not only possible but something people eagerly sought. The growth of multicultural meeting places (cities) made the exchange of ideas even more common. Although tribal identifications (nations) remained, intertribal communication flourished.

Postmodernism became possible with global communication, especially as a result of the incredible tool of the internet. Social media makes it theoretically possible to contact anyone in the world at any time. A worldwide community of sorts has developed, adding another layer of epistemological complexity to existing tribal groups as well as nation-states and their cities. Ironically, this global community makes possible an ultraindividualism that takes innovative thinking to new heights in terms of creativity and freedom. In such a setting the community-enabling power of religion is simultaneously threatened and made even more important. At their best the religions model how to create local communities out of the global one.

The question becomes whether the religious communities of the world can step up to the challenges created by this new way of thinking. What is religion becoming in order to meet this challenge? What does it need to become? And what is the role of the student-scholar in making that happen?

Why I Study Religion

RITA M. GROSS, UNIVERSITY OF WISCONSIN, EAU CLAIRE

An only child, I grew up in both cultural and economic poverty on a marginal dairy farm in northern Wisconsin. Not being allowed to play with neighborhood kids and with no books, telephone, or television in our house, I had to rely on my own resources for companionship. Animals, nature, and my own mind supplied that companionship. School was easy for me, and I loved to read and explore as much as I could within the limitations of a library system that refused to loan me books because my parents lived just over the county line. Then there was the conservative church my parents attended, which further censored reading and learning possibilities as much as it could.

I had a lot of time to think and a great deal of provocation to do so, given the narrowness and limitations of my cultural world. I was always interested in deeper questions concerning the meaning and purpose of life and did not like disciplines in which one was expected primarily to reproduce already available information rather than engage in introspection and speculation. Hence my freshman-year rejection of a college teacher's recommendation that I should pursue a degree in one of the sciences simply because I excelled in a difficult course. I said I wanted to major in a discipline that embraced thinking about issues; I was going to major in philosophy.

It turned out that philosophy was not satisfying to me in the long run. Despite my negative experiences with the religion in which I was reared, I was more interested in religion than in philosophy. My university did not offer a degree in religious studies, but I took as many courses in the philosophy of religion as I could. As a student with a very high grade point average, which was rare in the early 1960s, I was targeted for graduate school despite being a female. I decided I did not want to continue studying philosophy because it seemed to me that philosophy was almost completely cerebral and didn't really deal with deep, existential questions of life and death. Religion was the field in which those questions were asked and considered. So I resolved to pursue a PhD in religious studies, despite advice from a favorite woman professor, who tried to warn me that a woman would not be accepted in that field.

In my senior year of college (1964–65), I made another very important decision, perhaps the most important decision of my life. I had already decided to pursue a degree studying religion, not philosophy. But I also realized that I did not want to limit my study to Western religions. I wanted to study how people had asked and answered questions about life's imponderables, and there was no reason to assume that the religions of my own culture had come up with all of the interesting answers to those questions.

That is how and why I went off to the Divinity School of the University of Chicago in 1965 to study a field they called "the history of religions," then headed by Mircea Eliade, who was at the height of his fame. I quickly passed required entry-level exams, which mainly covered Western religions, and decided that my language of choice would be Sanskrit. Everyone enrolled in the history of religions program had to study a language connected to their specialty; I decided on Sanskrit because, at that point in time, the United States did not have diplomatic relations with China and it did not then look as if one would ever be able to study Chinese religions in China, whereas the situation was different with India. In the long run, however, that decision probably had more to do with my "karmic connection" with all things Indian, which I was not aware of at that time.

However, I hadn't counted on what it was like to be the only woman in an all-male classroom. I realized immediately that the professors did not take the few women students seriously. The student body at the divinity school numbered about four hundred, and twelve of us were women, six of whom had entered that same fall. Our professors censored what they taught due to the presence of women and worried out loud about what they were going to do with "all these women who now want to study religion." As a child, I hated being a girl because I could clearly see that my gender imposed limitations on my life. As is common in such cases, I experienced a great deal of self-hatred, but as a teenager, I also experienced something else that was literally lifesaving. One day, I had a very clear, sudden realization: there's nothing wrong with being a girl. It's the system!

In my second year of graduate school, I wrote a paper on the role of women in one of the religions we were studying. My purpose was very clear. I wanted to find out if things are as bad for women in other places as they are in Western religions. Instead of getting an answer to that question, I found that Western scholars were not at all interested in what women did or thought religiously—a very important, though painful discovery to make in 1967, when second-wave feminism was not yet well established. However, Eliade, for whom I had written the paper, praised my work and suggested I should continue this work in my doctoral dissertation. My reply to him is quite instructive in terms of how women had been socialized to think of themselves in the 1950s and 1960s. "No," I said. "I want to do my dissertation on something important." I eventually changed my mind, which is how I became one of the earliest feminist scholars of religion, though my time in graduate school was made miserable by some faculty members because of that decision. I was told by one of my mentors that, as an intelligent person, I should understand that the generic masculine covered and included the feminine, making it unnecessary to study women specifically.

The one piece still missing in how and why I study religion concerns how I came to focus so much on Buddhism. The causal incident occurred just after I moved to Eau Claire in 1973 to begin teaching there. In the midst of great personal suffering, I simply had a "road to Damascus" experience concerning the truth of Buddhism as I was preparing a lecture on the Four Noble Truths. Even later, in 1980, speaking as a Buddhist, I became involved in interreligious dialogue, hoping to heal some of the wounds left by my early training in a cruel and intolerant form of Christianity. That brings my story full circle and explains the genesis of my major approaches to religions and the study of religions. I care about methodologies concerning how to study religions, which, I claim, must always include cross-cultural perspectives— about feminist perspectives on religion, about Buddhism, and especially about gender and Buddhism. As a Buddhist critical and constructive thinker and now a Buddhist dharma teacher, I also care about what a viable and relevant Western Buddhism will look like, and I care intensely about how to flourish in a world characterized by religious diversity.

8

New Trajectories for the Study of Religion

The psychological, social, philosophical, and religious changes I have been talking about in the course of this book indicate that we are in the midst of a new trajectory for the nature of global religion in the twenty-first century. Not only is religion becoming more independent of state control, but a global form of religion is developing that depends more on internet-based virtual movements than brick-and-mortar religious institutions. Individuals and their interpretations of religion rival traditional statements of what it means to be religious within a certain tradition. All of this is taking place in the context of three social challenges to religion: religion used for terroristic purposes, the challenge of transcendent religion by the secular religions of atheism and agnosticism, and a worldwide antireligion movement that seeks to further the Enlightenment project of replacing prophetic religion with human social engineering. Both the new trajectory of religion and these challenges demand the attention of religious studies scholars.

As the nature of global religion changes, the ways in which we study it must also change. Every good scientist knows that scholarly tools must change and develop as the subject matter of research changes. One cannot measure atomic particles with a yardstick; to get inside the atom scientists had to develop electron microscopes and cyclotrons for that purpose. New scholarly tools and methodologies for religious studies are inevitable. As for religion, one wonders to what extent the traditional ways of studying religion (using history, phenomenology, functionalism, and structuralism) must also change. The older methods, at least as they are practiced, seem unable to cope with the speed of change and dynamism exhibited by the newer, more fluid forms of religion that are developing. Research tools and methods that scholars can use to study fluidity and flexibility will need to come alongside the traditional methods, which work best in the study of essences, psychological dynamics, and historical precedents.

If both religion and the methods used to study it are undergoing change, then it stands to reason that the nature of being a student of religion will also change, meaning that the student of religion is also on a new trajectory. For starters, students of religion have more religious information available to them than at any other point in time. Knowledge about Korean shamanism is a click away. Want to know about Branch Davidians in Waco, Texas, and what they believe? Google it. In addition to the quantity of knowledge, access to that knowledge is more widespread. A person does not have to be near a great library to study religion; he or she needs only the internet. By using social media, religious people around the world and the scholars who study them can be contacted almost at will. Collecting information about world religions is infinitely easier today, which allows the student to concentrate on the equally important tasks of interpretation and application.

Thus we are faced with three new trajectories: global religion, religious studies methodology, and what these trajectories mean for students of religion. While these are actually subtrajectories of a single trajectory, for heuristic purposes it is helpful to comment on each of them in turn to get a fuller idea of what is happening.

The New Trajectory of Religion in the World: Religion Good and Bad

One of the most helpful Christian theological adjustments I made as a budding student of religion came as a result of reading Karl Barth's

Church Dogmatics when I was a senior in college. At the urging of one of my professors (a Barth scholar), I did an independent study with him that simply entailed reading large sections of the *Dogmatics* and discussing what I learned. It was a rich time that confirmed my plans to attend theological school after my undergraduate work.

I remember well the day we were discussing what I had been reading about Barth's views of religion. *Church Dogmatics* includes sections in which Barth outlines what he thinks of the category that I have been calling "religion." The most pointed thing he says is from *Church Dogmatics*, his essential point being that all religions, even Christianity, are human creations, not divine revelation.[1] They are human efforts to reach out and touch God. And because they are human creations, they are fallible. Very fallible.

I knew that when Barth first articulated this view in a debate concerning general revelation with another European theologian, Emil Brunner, Barth's view was interpreted as a criticism of religious studies.[2] Brunner said that the study of religion, since it is a part of God's general revelation to humankind, could lead to a better understanding of Christian special revelation. Barth voiced an emphatic "no" (*nein*) to this view. If the study of religion is expected to lead to revelation, it is idolatry, since all religions, including Christianity, are human creations and therefore not to be trusted as revelation. When I first read about this debate, however, I did not see it as a criticism of religious studies.

As a young Baptist college student, a son of a Baptist minister, and someone dedicated to the Baptist church and all it stood for, this was an amazing insight. It rocked my world, as the young people are wont to say these days. I not only read Barth's ideas and did my best to understand what it was he was saying and why, but I also realized immediately that it was true (though you, dear reader, may want me to qualify that statement by saying "true for me"). To put it more precisely, I realized that it made enormous sense and seemed true at

---

1. Karl Barth, *Church Dogmatics*, II/2, section 17 (Edinburgh: T&T Clark, 1936–77), as quoted and summarized in R. J. Plantinga, *Christianity and Plurality: Classic and Contemporary Readings* (Oxford: Blackwell, 1999), 223.

2. For a fresh look at Emil Brunner and this debate with Barth, see Alister McGrath, *Emil Brunner: A Reappraisal* (Chichester, UK: Wiley-Blackwell, 2014).

the time. As the years have passed, I have come to embrace Barth's "no" as a cornerstone of my vocation, that is, the study of religion. The religions of the world, even Christianity, are human creations and need to be studied as such.

This insight has helped me in several ways. It made sense of the approach religious studies scholars take to their craft, which is not a study of prophetic religion or a study of religion as a disease but a study of natural religion. In that moment, I understood Max Müller's statement that the subject matter of the science of religion is natural religion.[3] Barth gave me a strong theological warrant for studying religion as natural—a human creation. One needn't eschew the whole of Christian theology in order to study "natural" religion.

The realization that religion is a human creation also gave me some categories I needed to account for what I was discovering in my study of religion. Not all religion is good. Some of it is bad. The religious naysayers, beginning with Karl Marx and Sigmund Freud and continuing with Daniel Dennet and Sam Harris and Richard Dawkins, were not just concocting stories about the deleterious effects religion can have. Although they did misconstrue religion in essential ways by being absolute in their views of negative religion, they certainly were not making up the evidence in order to show that religion can be used for evil purposes.

A student of religion does not have to get very far in his or her studies to see these negative effects. Even in one's own tradition (which for most Western readers is Christianity), a person can see negative expressions of religion—ways of thinking, feeling, and doing religion that do not lead to human flourishing and are actually false to the real teachings of the religion in question. Barth helped me deal with that. In so doing he helped me more effectively understand and confront where some of the possible side roads the current trajectory of global religion may take us.

Consider two examples. Let's begin with religious persecution. As we study human history we clearly see that the various religions of the world have always experienced some level of persecution. In the past, however, the persecution has almost always come from people who

---

3. See introduction to this book.

STUDY AID

RELIGION AND HUMAN RIGHTS EXERCISE

1. Although all religions have a view of human rights, not all religions have the same view. Three issues divide the religions' views of human rights:

   human nature
   role of religion in society
   content of specific human rights

   For each of these three issues, first write a description of the issue; then compare and contrast two different religious views of each issue.

2. Compare the Christian view of human rights with the Confucian view of human rights. How might the contrasts in these views affect the interactions that modern-day China has with the United States in political, economic, and social interactions? Do you think it is necessary to create a third view of human rights, taking the best and most essential of both the Christian and Confucian, in order to facilitate conversations between the two?

From Terry Muck, Harold Netland, and Gerald McDermott, eds., *Handbook of Religion* (Grand Rapids: Baker Academic, 2014), 777.

---

are championing another religion, a competitor, so to speak. While this form of persecution—we'll call it "competitor persecution"—still exists in the world, another form of persecution, equally dangerous, has emerged. This second form of persecution comes from those who are attacking religion in general. They are not the champions of a competitor religion; they are the champions of no religion at all. We'll call this form of persecution "antireligion persecution."

Consider a second, related example that comes from scholars of religion themselves. Most scholars of religion approach their study using the methodology of a related social science, such as psychology, sociology, anthropology, philosophy, and so on. Sometimes these psychologists of religion, sociologists of religion, anthropologists of religion, and philosophers of religion conclude that religion itself is nothing more than a manifestation of psychology, sociology, anthropology, or philosophy. That is, they conclude that there is nothing unique about religion once the manifestations of religious behavior have been accounted for by these other disciplines. Scholars of religion have become accustomed to describing this phenomena as the *reduction* of religion, that is, once religious behavior has been accounted for psychologically or sociologically, there is really nothing left to study. There is nothing sui generis about religion—no unique content that simply uses the rationale of religion as a rubric.

Both the antireligion and the reduction of religion movements are side roads that can distract the student of religion from his or her scholarly task. Both can be effectively argued against using almost self-evident evidence from the religions themselves, but one should not underestimate the importance of both the antireligion movement in cultures at large and the reduction of religion movement within religious studies itself.[4]

A New Trajectory for the Student of Religion: The Global Scholar

Part of what it means to be a student of religion these days involves developing a proficiency in adopting a global outlook on one's studies that complements rather than replaces a local outlook. It is necessary to be able to study a religion as it appears in one's hometown and local church—or any "hometown" and "local church." It is necessary and even essential to be able to do that kind of study, but it is not enough. One must also be able to connect that specific manifestation of religion with the global expression of that religion and the global expression of religion in general. To be a "global student" of religion these days demands an awareness of worldwide expressions of religion as the context of whatever one is studying at the time.

In 1977–78 I lived in Sri Lanka, doing research for my doctoral dissertation on Buddhist monasticism. I visited Buddhist monasteries

---

4. The "almost self-evident" evidence to which I refer comes in several forms. One is the argument put forward by Rudolf Otto in *The Idea of the Holy*, trans. John W. Harvey (1917; repr., New York: Oxford University Press, 1958) that humans tend to have universally similar experiences of the holy—we might call this existential evidence. Another is the argument from evidences of the positive effects of religion on human flourishing. Robert Woodberry, in "Missionary Roots of Liberal Democracy," *American Political Science Review* 106, no. 2 (2012): 244–74, has produced sociological evidence of this sort—we might call this social scientific evidence. Finally, biological evidence is being produced that traces religious traits such as worship, altruism, and meditation to biological functions.

and interviewed Buddhist *bhikkhus* (monks) about how closely they followed the centuries-old Buddhist monastic rule, the *Vinaya Pitaka*.[5] The dominant point that emerged and became a central feature of my dissertation was that Buddhist *bhikkhus* generally said they followed the rule in detail, though our discussions indicated that few of them did in practice. New cultural conditions and the practicalities of modern and postmodern life meant that they had new, sometimes unspoken rules that allowed them to cope with cenobitic life. They lived by the spirit of the *Vinaya Pitaka* but not its letter.

Those visits and interviews were the ostensible reason for my living in Sri Lanka for two years, and from a purely research point of view it was a successful trip. But I have often said that as satisfying and successful as that part of my international trip was, I probably learned more about "religious studies" (and life) from living in a culture where I was a minority in almost every way—ethnically, culturally, religiously. While I still had definite privileges as an American in that era, I lived with a Sinhalese family; I ate at their table, participated in family affairs to some degree, observed the working life of the father (he was a government official), and watched their two teenage children navigate a series of crises not all that different from those in the life of an American teenager.

And on Sunday mornings we attended a Buddhist "church." One of my professors at Northwestern University had alerted me to this phenomenon in Sri Lanka. Having done research in Sri Lanka for his dissertation, he studied in some detail what he called the "protestantization" of Sri Lanka Buddhism.[6] His thesis was that the Christian mission effort in Sri Lanka had the unintended consequence of changing the way Sri Lankan Buddhists, especially in urban areas, practiced their Buddhism. The purpose of the mission itself—to plant Christian churches and convert Buddhists to Christianity—was only marginally successful. But Buddhists in Sri Lanka began to borrow some Christian organizational practices and ways of being Buddhist

---

5. See my dissertation, Terry C. Muck, *A Comparison of the Pali Vinaya Pitaka and St. Basil's Longer and Shorter Rules* (PhD diss., University of Michigan, 1977), microfilm.

6. George Bond, *The Buddhist Revival in Sri Lanka: Religious Tradition, Reinterpretation, and Response* (Columbia: University of South Carolina Press, 1988).

that were remarkably similar to what the Christian missionaries were trying to establish.

For example, the Buddhist "church" we attended on Sunday mornings was held in a meeting hall with pews. The leader gave a lecture, in English, on a Buddhist teaching. We met for an hour. We had a "potluck" luncheon after the meeting. We met people and talked about who we were and what we were doing in Sri Lanka. The other people who attended were from the social class represented by the family that my wife and I were living with: governmental officials, business owners, and persons in the travel industry. In terms of being Buddhist, it was obvious that they were "all in." But it was equally obvious that attending a Buddhist temple, offering incense, and listening to a *bhikkhu* chanting *pirit* was not the way they wanted to practice their faith, or at least they didn't want to do that exclusively. They wanted to think about their religion in a way that they had been taught by the Christians doing church in their midst, particularly the Protestant variety of church.

It was an interesting situation for me to be in. Since my professor had studied this manifestation of religion as a movement, I wanted to observe it. I also wanted to participate along with my host family as a way of learning more about what it meant to be Buddhist in a former colony of the British Empire. At the same time, I wanted to study temple Buddhism—"real Buddhism," as I remember identifying it to myself at the time. In the back of my mind I considered this form of Buddhism to be the most important; this is what my friends and colleagues back home would really want to hear about. It was, after all, what I had trained back home to study. I had come to Sri Lanka to observe it firsthand. Only in retrospect did I see that I was observing the kinds of religious exchanges that were happening everywhere. As part of the development of global religion, movements borrow from, exchange with, and imitate one another all over the world. Even if the beliefs don't change very much, the practices and ways of being religious do.

What I experienced was the first glimmers of postmodern religion emerging. As I look back on that time, I understand better what was happening to me (at a subconscious level): I was learning what it meant to be a global student of religion. Not a student who simply absorbs the ways in which Western universities teach us to be students of religion but a student who has seen firsthand the way postmodernism changes the way people around the world embrace their religions intellectually and emotionally. Because of those changes in thought and affect, they develop new religious practices to match their globalized ways of thinking and being.

In short, I was becoming a global student of religion. In the years since, I have often asked myself whether these insights and lessons could have come in any other way.

A New Trajectory for the Study of Religion: The Introduction to World Religions Course

It may be that the changes outlined in the previous two sections of this chapter demand that we rethink the staples of religious studies pedagogy. What are these staples? They include classroom teaching, especially the lecture; content intentionally shorn of emotions, commitment, and expressed beliefs; critical thinking applied to transcendent truth; and the survey of world religions course that you may be taking right now. I would like to use the Introduction to World Religions course to discuss the elements of religious studies pedagogy that I just mentioned. It is possible that the way in which the survey course is taught—both its content and teaching methods—needs to be rethought.

Full disclosure: I have taught the Introduction to World Religions course for over a quarter of a century. I love the course. It is a way of introducing new religion students to a field of study that I find fascinating. In teaching the course, I follow the pattern of teaching that is common to religious studies programs. Essentially, I attempt to introduce students to the history, beliefs, and practices of nine or ten world religions, which are designated as world religions because they have successfully crossed cultural boundaries in their historic spread. I start in India with Hinduism, Buddhism, Jainism (sometimes), and Sikhism. Then I move on to China and Confucianism and Taoism, making a quick stop in Japan for Shintoism and then moving on to the Middle East for Judaism, Christianity, and Islam. Perhaps if there is time (i.e., a fifteen-week semester instead of a twelve-week quarter), I add a lecture on indigenous religions and one on new religious movements, noting that a survey course on each is available to complement the material covered in the World Religions course.

As I said, I have taught this course many times. I almost always use the latest edition of *A History of the World's Religions*[7] as my primary text. To that I add a few primary sources—*The Bhagavad Gita*,[8] *Dhammapada*,[9] *The Analects*,[10] *Tao Te Ching*[11] are staples—to give students a taste of what the religions "sound like" in the original. I devote the first week to introductory material on the study of religion, which includes some demographics, and then spend one week studying each religion for the course of the semester. We traditionally meet either two times per week (for one and a half hours) or three times per week (for one-hour periods). I lecture, working my way through a three-part outline for each religion: part one covers history; part two is teachings; and part three is practices. I give two exams—a midterm on Eastern religions and a test on Western religions at the end of the term. The students like the course. I like the course. But toward the end of my teaching career I began to think about ways the course could be made better by making it more appropriate to the changing world of religion. My thoughts have led me to consider three general changes. Let's look at each in turn and consider why they may be necessary.

Change One: From World Religions to World Religion

This one is deceptively simple. What if we changed the title of the course by removing the *s* from *religions* so that the previous title, Introduction to World Religions, becomes Introduction to World Religion? Although the change may seem minor, the implication is huge. While the change asserts a number of things, the primary

7. The most recent is the thirteenth edition: David Noss and Blake Grongaard, *A History of the World's Religions* (Upper Saddle River, NJ: Pearson, 2011).
8. *The Bhagavad Gita*, trans. Laurie Patton (London: Penguin Books, 2008).
9. *Dhammapada*, trans. Juan Mascaró (Harmondsworth, UK: Penguin Books, 1973).
10. Confucius, *The Analects*, trans. D. C. Lau (New York: Penguin Books, 1979).
11. Lao Tzu, *Tao Te Ching*, trans. D. C. Lau (London: Penguin Books, 1964).

implication is that the presence of religions in the world indicates that a basic human category of behavior called religion exists. It takes into account the historical fact that all people, everywhere, at all times have been religious and that the few experiments in history that have attempted to excise religious expression from human behavior have failed miserably.[12] Since religion in general is a universal human category of behavior, it is worthy of scholarly study.

Some see this recognition of universal human religion as one more nail in the coffin of exclusivistic religion—that only one of the world's religions deserves to be called a religion; the rest are impostors. I do not believe that is what it means. One can assert the belief in one's own religion as the best without doing away with respect for other religious expressions. What the recognition of universal human religion does do is move away from the privileging of the ten so-called world religions as the main expressions of human religiosity. It also acknowledges that human religious expression in any given context is much more complex than devotion to one religion, which leads us to change two.

Change Two: From World Religions to Indigenous/ World/New Religious Movements

None of the world religions exists in any real human cultural setting without being dramatically influenced by two other powerful religious forces—indigenous religions, which have been the basis of most societies since ancient times, and new religious movements, which have come into being as a result of postmodernism and its reactions with modernism and premodernism. In chapter 6 I discussed anthropologist Clifford Geertz's discovery of this in his studies of Indonesian and Moroccan Islam. Though there is no question that he was observing the religion of Islam in both Indonesia and Morocco, Islam looked quite different in each place as a result of different indigenous religious backgrounds and the way in which new religious movements had developed.

If we want to study "religion" rather than "religions," it is better to acknowledge that in any given setting all three manifestations of

12. The most recent large-scale attempts are the Marxist-Stalinist approach in the Soviet Union and the Maoist approach in China. Neither worked.

religion—world religion, indigenous religion, and new religious movements—must be accounted for. The boiling down of religions to their essences can still be achieved, but it is better done at the end of one's introduction to world religion rather than at the starting point. What that means for the actual teaching of this course brings us to change three.

Change Three: Balancing Content with Process

None of these changes advocates doing away with studying the content of the historic world religions, especially Hinduism, Buddhism, Confucianism, Christianity, and Islam. That information is still vital to the course. But significant time must be spent in each case showing what Geertz discovered—that the world religions take dramatically different forms in different cultures and that it is impossible to predict what form each religion will take as it establishes roots in new places.

The student of religion must be taught not only religious content but also the process of exegeting a culture's religious expressions, identifying how Islam, for example, is taking shape in a particular place. This calls for more than lectures; at least some measure of field-based learning must take place. This can be accomplished with something as simple as having the students visit a new mosque in a historically Christian neighborhood, after which they are asked to make observations and then answer the question, *How does what is happening in this mosque compare with the lecture on essential Islam?*

These three changes should be considered by anyone who teaches the course and by those who take it. Whether we adjust the way in which the course is being taught by just a little or a lot depends on how important we consider each of the three rationales for change to be. At the very least we should acknowledge that religious expression in the world today is much more complex and diverse than it has ever been. The student of religion must be aware of that complexity as he or she undertakes the study of religion.

Conclusion

The changing status of religion in the world today can be seen in different ways. Some may see it as a challenge to the entire discipline of religious studies. Although the denigration of religion and religious people may tempt us to focus on the pathological aspects of religion more than the evidence warrants, this particular challenge can also motivate the student of religion to get it right. One does not have to be religious to be fair and just to people who are religious.

These challenges, however, can be seen in a more positive light. Beyond providing a defense of religion, the study of religion contributes to human flourishing. The religions of the world and the religious people of the world make the world a better place in which to live—a truth that the student-scholar of religion comes to see more clearly than anyone else. Through our research and study we preserve the miracle of religious belief for future generations.

Why I Study Religion

JUDITH BERLING, GRADUATE THEOLOGICAL UNION

When I was eleven years old, my family moved to Dubuque, Iowa. In 1956 Dubuque was a small city of fifty thousand people. It was so overwhelmingly Roman Catholic that the church there had an archbishop. We were Presbyterian and thus part of a religious minority; all Protestants in pre-Vatican II Dubuque knew why they were Protestant and what that meant. The theological disputes of the Reformation were alive and well in Dubuque. Though a minority, Protestants were represented and anchored by both a Lutheran and a Presbyterian seminary. My church was across the street from the Presbyterian seminary, and my Sunday school teachers were seminary professors. Needless to say, our Sunday school experience was theologically "meatier" than most. I was deeply immersed in religious and theological issues from the time I entered puberty.

In college during the early and mid-1960s, I encountered the fruits of Vatican II, engaged in experimental worship (agape meals and the like) of the early 1960s liturgical movement, and strongly considered seminary, in part because of the involvement of churches and clergy in the civil rights movement and the anti–Vietnam War movement. As I saw it, the "action" seemed to be in the churches. For two years I was involved in a student ministry for a small United Church of Christ church in rural Minnesota that lacked an ordained pastor. It was an experience in that parish that drew me into the study and teaching of religion.

One Sunday in my second year in the parish I took a Japanese Christian friend with me to church. The parishioners did not know what to make of him, and some of them even panicked (one person called him a "Jap"). I knew these were fundamentally good people, but they had never met anyone of Asian background, and they had been influenced by anti-war propaganda about the Vietnamese. Deeply shaken, I realized that my real vocation was in the classroom and in scholarship, committing myself to the study of Asian religions, knowledge of Asian languages, and firsthand experience of the culture and its writings so that I could help fellow Americans understand Asian peoples and their beliefs and practices. I believed that Asian religions were important keys to understanding those cultures in their distinctiveness, complemented by Asian literature and history.

Two major themes have dominated my study of Chinese and Japanese religions and cultures. The first is the pattern of religious inclusivism (multiple religious participation), as opposed to a dominant pattern of religious exclusivism in the Christian West. The second has been to understand more deeply what is entailed in coming to understand another religious world rather than simply learning facts about it. I see both as developments of my deep interest in the study of religions as a means to pursue cross-cultural understanding.

Conclusion

In 1986 Eric Sharpe finished revising and updating his fine book *Comparative Religion: A History*. He ends the work with this observation:

> I am not going to be so rash as to identify [religious studies] as an art or a science; it contains elements of both. But it certainly involves the mastery of a craft. To listen is an art; to grasp what [religious people] are saying involves both a craft and a science. But unless the student feels the force of arguments on more than one side, it is likely that a point somewhere has been missed.[1]

Whether religious studies is an art or a science or a craft is worth debating; that it involves a great deal of hard work is not. The student who chooses to study religion in all of its human manifestations is dedicating him- or herself to as much work as any discipline demands. In addition to the almost inevitable study of languages (more than one language is typically necessary) and the mastery of research skills, the student of religion is called on to be a superior listener, a tolerant conversation partner, a more than curious onlooker into ways of life strange and foreign, and a restrained evaluator of other ways of

---

1. Eric Sharpe, *Comparative Religion: A History*, 2nd ed. (London: Duckworth, 1986), 319.

living—all in the interest of human flourishing. Is being a religious studies scholar worth all that? I say yes.

I say this based on my own experience as a scholar of religion, of course. As you have probably concluded from what I have said thus far in the book, I find religious studies to be a rewarding vocation. It satisfies my curious personality, gives me reasons to read and travel that might not have otherwise occurred, and makes me feel like I have, in a small way, made a contribution to the flourishing of my fellow human beings. From the perspective of my own past, I can say without equivocation that the study of religion is a good thing to do—even if you, a new student of religion, never take another course in religion.

But you need more than that. You need some evidence and some assurances that the study of religion is worth the hard work. You need evidence that it will make a difference not only in your life but also in the world around you. I imagine that those of you who go further in religious studies would very much like some assurances that the hours of study and days and weeks of field-based research and years of dedication will bring you to the place I now find myself—looking back on a career well spent. Can I argue that you will experience the same satisfaction if you decide to study religion—whether you decide to study just one course in world religion, occasional courses here and there, an ongoing reading program, an advanced degree, or even a commitment to religious studies as a vocation?

Maybe, maybe not. The reason for my tentative response is that such an argument rests, at least in part, on the discipline and value of religious studies—not just its current value but its future value. Predicting the future course of an academic discipline is not an easy matter, and I would contend that it is especially difficult in a field like religious studies. Religion in the world is under a sustained attack, the likes of which has not been seen since the days of the Enlightenment disparagers—the ones Friedrich Schleiermacher calls religion's "cultured despisers."[2] It may not be logical to think that the growing unpopularity of religion makes those who choose to study it also unpopular, but there may be more than a little truth to that conclusion.

---

2. From the subtitle of his *On Religion: Speeches to Its Cultured Despisers* (1799; repr., Cambridge: Cambridge University Press, 1996).

But it's not just a matter of popularity. There is more to it than that. As we have seen, religion and religious practice itself are undergoing some dramatic changes in the world today, and it is hard to predict what those changes will mean for the student of religion. It will certainly mean that you, as a beginning student of religion, will have a different experience—should you choose to continue your studies in some form—than I have had. You will study virtual religions, global syncretisms, hybrid religious personalities, internet-based religious promotions, and religious change taking place at the speed of light, all of which I knew nothing about in 1977 when I graduated from Northwestern University with a PhD in the History and Literature of Religion. You will talk to people I don't know exist, using methodologies I can barely understand, and addressing cultural problems so complex that figuring out where culture ends and religion begins is almost impossible.

Some intrepid souls periodically venture opinions on "the future of religious studies." Rosemary Radford Ruether, for example, argues that unless the role of women in religious studies is acknowledged the discipline is headed for disaster. Ursula King agrees but adds two more challenges—postmodern thinking and the varied forms of spiritual practice. Some are convinced that the adversarial and/ or complementary roles of theology and religious studies have never been fully argued to the ground (I would make that argument), and others cling to the idea, despite all evidence to the contrary, that religion is doomed to wither away entirely as humankind evolves to higher and higher levels of consciousness (an argument I would never make, based on the current phenomenon of religious growth). Perhaps the safest thing to say about the "future of religious studies" is that it will be different.

However, I think it is an incontrovertible fact that, in the future, religious studies will be no less important than it is today. It may be even more important.

While religion has always been important to individual human beings and their communities, *why* it is important has evolved. The role it played (and plays) in primitive cultures is different than the role it played and plays in modern cultures. It seems self-evident that the role it is playing and will play in cultures influenced by postmodern thinking will also change. As a shorthand way of describing these changes, I like to say that religion has gone from being an identity marker to a meaning-maker to a community builder.[3] Perhaps it is most accurate to say that today and in the future religion will continue to play all three roles. Let me remind you of these three roles one more time.

As an identity marker for primitive peoples religion acknowledged and reinforced tribal membership. Meaning was almost totally a result of being a member of the tribe, and no community needed to be built. Community was synonymous with tribal membership and was arguably the most important thing about belonging. If anything needed to be understood and underscored it was the role of individuals in this tight-knit band. Religions associated with these tribal structures (called indigenous religions and also tribal, archaic, and primitive religions) still exist both in dominant and recessive social forms.

Indigenous religions and their emphasis on community membership are still important today, though usually in a recessive social form. While indigenous religions are less and less evident as practiced religions, and as modern and postmodern ways of thinking come to dominate more and more cultures, some of the elements of indigenous religions can aid urban, postmodern cultures in which community building is not a strength, though it remains the predominant need. The "bowling alone" phenomenon, where people spend more and more time in individual pursuits and less and less time in communal activities, indicates to most observers a weakness of postmodern living.

Religion is one of the last human associations that exists primarily to provide community. The well-known canard that the Christian church is the last human institution that exists primarily for the benefit of nonmembers illustrates the religion's importance as a community builder. As globalization and social media tout the so-called community provided by Facebook (masking what might be more accurately called "parallel individualism"), the importance of religion—to the extent that it can and does provide real community—grows.

Religion's potential as an antidote to the excessive individualism of modernism—given the freedoms inherent to most cultures in the West

3. See chaps. 3, 4, and 5.

that value human rights—increases its importance but also presents a downside. Excessive freedom breeds anxiety, and this anxiety seems especially pronounced when it comes to discerning the meaning of life. As pluralistic democracies make viable more acceptable answers to the question *Why do I exist?*, choosing from among these answers becomes problematic. Excessive freedom breeds anxiety because it fails in the essential human task of meaning-making. Religion helps fill that gap.

I am guessing that few of us today would say that we belong to a tribe—but perhaps we need to. Even fewer of us would acknowledge that the freedoms we enjoy, or at least aspire to, are excessive, but if having to make endless choices from among countless options creates anxiety, how can we demur? It might be better to embrace a religion that gives us some guidance. Being in contact with people almost incessantly, both literally and virtually, few of us would say that we are short of community, but perhaps we are. And perhaps religion can help fill our need for *genuine* community.

It may sound like I am beginning to preach here, and I probably am. I do believe religion is a positive force for human good. But my intention in this short book is to advocate the study of religion, not religion itself. And that I do with relish. Each of these benefits of religion—identity marker, meaning-maker, and community builder—is eminently researchable in today's world. Not only is the research possible, but it is also important. Taken together, these benefits help fashion a strong answer to the question *Why study religion?*

Why I Study Religion

ARVIND SHARMA, MCGILL UNIVERSITY

How I got into the study of religion may not be an edifying story, but it is perhaps an interesting one. The story starts in the dusty districts of Gujarat where I served from 1962 to 1968 as a member of the Indian Administrative Service (the IAS for short), which was the successor to the ICS (the Indian Civil Service)—the "steel frame" of the British Raj.

In other words, I was professionally as far removed from the study of religion as one can get.

In 1968 I was admitted into the doctoral program in economics at the Maxwell School of Citizenship and Public Affairs at Syracuse University in upstate New York, still removed from the study of religion. That was to change. The question that set new forces in motion was: What subject should I choose for my dissertation? The department wanted me to write my dissertation on some formal academic topic in the field of economics, get my degree, get a job, and get on with my life. But I had not decided to study economics just to get a degree. I had, admittedly naively, chosen to pursue higher studies in economics to find out what makes countries prosperous or keeps them poor so that I might help rid India of poverty. As if this was not subversive enough, I began to entertain the idea that noneconomic factors play a far greater role, at least in some societies, in promoting economic development and growth than economic ones. It seemed to me that religion is one such noneconomic factor affecting economic development. The department, although it did not oppose this line of thought, was not entirely sympathetic. During a meeting with the head of the department I found him musing that they had no one who could supervise this kind of work, and that I also had no degree in religious studies to pursue this line of inquiry.

This turned out to be a decisive moment. In effect, I responded by saying that not having anyone to supervise my work was the department's problem but not having a degree in the study of religion was mine. I decided to take care of it.

I discovered that Harvard Divinity School offered a Masters in Theological Studies degree, which seemed tailor-made for my requirements. I applied for admission and was accepted. Once I arrived, a whole new intellectual world opened up to me that I had not even known existed. This was the world of the academic study of religion. I was, of course, familiar with the study *of* religion in India; India's ethos of plurality ensured that I knew as much about Islamic *madrasas* and Christian seminaries as about Hindu *maṭhas* and Buddhist *vihāras*. But study *about* religion as I saw it being carried out at Harvard was unknown to me.

I never looked back. The degree in economics fell by the wayside even as my mother demanded to know why I was at the divinity school and not at the business school. I also let go of my job in India, from which I was on leave, to the consternation of friends and foes alike. To freely study beliefs without having to believe in them, to study practices without having to practice them, and to study worldviews without necessarily subscribing to them, utilizing not just one but an array of methods had, for me, an intoxicating quality about it. The possibility that skepticism need not turn into sourness but can become inquiry; that agnosticism need not lead to pessimism but could encourage new explorations; that aporias need not make us tear out our hair in frustration but can fill us with wonder; and that the plurality of religions need not be perceived as entities posing a threat to one another, but rather as entities reciprocally illuminating one another, provided a horizon toward which I could travel forever. I have been traveling ever since.

APPENDIX 1

Classic Books in the Study of Religion

In its short century and a half of existence, religious studies has produced its share of classic works. Below are eleven of them. According to David Tracy, *classic* means that these texts have an "excess of meaning."[1] An "excess of meaning" means two things: the work can be read and reread by the same reader, with each reading offering additional value from the reading, and the work has inherent value to persons of other cultures (i.e., cultures other than the one in which the book was written).

Notice that the books on this list have been written using at least eight methodologies from eight fields of study. Because religious studies is inherently interdisciplinary, in order to understand religious expression in any specific time and place multiple scholarly points of view must be utilized.

1. David Tracy, *The Analogical Imagination: Christian Theology and the Culture of Pluralism* (New York: Crossroad, 1978), 8.

Reading any one of the books below will further your under-standing of religious studies; reading all eleven would contribute to a self-directed introduction to the discipline.

Douglas, Mary. *Natural Symbols: Explorations in Cosmology*. 1970. Reprint, London: Routledge, 1996. (Anthropology)

Durkheim, Émile. *Elementary Forms of the Religious Life*. 1915. Reprint, New York: Free Press, 1995. (Sociology)

Frazer, James George. *The Golden Bough*. 1890. Abridged ed., Mine-ola, NY: Dover, 2002. (Anthropology)

James, William. *The Varieties of Religious Experience*. 1902. Reprint, Mineola, NY: Dover, 2002. (Psychology)

Jastrow, Morris. *The Study of Religion*. London: Walter Scott, 1901. (History)

Levi-Strauss, Claude. *The Savage Mind*. Chicago: University of Chi-cago Press, 1962. (Structuralism)

Otto, Rudolf. *The Idea of the Holy*. Translated by John W. Har-vey. 1917. Reprint, New York: Oxford University Press, 1958. (Phenomenology)

Sharpe, Eric. *Comparative Religion: A History*. 2nd ed. London: Duckworth, 1986. (Comparative)

Smith, Wilfred Cantwell. *The Meaning and End of Religion: A New Approach to the Religious Traditions of Mankind*. New York: Macmillan, 1962. (History)

van der Leeuw, Gerardus. *Religion in Essence and Manifestation*. 2 vols. Translated by J. E. Turner. 1938. Reprint, New York: Harper & Row, 1963. (Philosophy)

Wach, Joachim. *The Comparative Study of Religion*. New York: Columbia University Press, 1958. (Comparative)

APPENDIX 2

Classic Essays in the Study of Religion

Like the previous list of classic books in religious studies, this appendix provides a list of classic essays in religious studies. Reading any one of the essays below will further your understanding of religious studies; reading all ten would contribute to a self-directed introduction to the discipline.

Barth, Karl. *Church Dogmatics*, II/2, section 17. Edinburgh: T&T Clark, 1977. (Theology)

Bellah, Robert. "Religious Evolution." In *Beyond Belief: Essays on Religion in a Post-Traditional World*, 20–50. New York: Harper & Row, 1970. (Sociology)

Berlin, Isaiah. "The Hedgehog and the Fox." In *The Proper Study of Mankind*, 436–97. 1953. Reprint, New York: Farrar, Straus & Giroux, 2000. (Philosophy)

Eck, Diana. "The Image of God." In *Darshan: Seeing the Divine Image in India*, 16–22. New York: Columbia University Press, 1998. (The Arts)

Geertz, Clifford. "Religion as a Cultural System." In *The Interpretation of Cultures*, 87–125. New York: Fontana, 1974. (Anthropology/Ethnography)

James, William. "The Will to Believe." In *The Will to Believe, Human Immorality, and Other Essays in Popular Philosophy*, 1–15. 1896. Reprint, Mineola, NY: Dover, 1959. (Psychology)

Müller, Max. "Essay on the Science of Religion." In vol. 1 of *Chips from a German Workshop*, vii–xxxiii. 1869. Reprint, Chico, CA: Scholars Press, 1985. (Science of Religion)

Smith, Jonathan Z. "The End of Comparison: Redescription and Rectification." In *A Magic Still Dwells*, edited by Kimberley Patton and Benjamin Ray. Berkeley: University of California Press, 2000. (History)

Wach, Joachim. "Development, Meaning, and Method in the Comparative Study of Religion." In *The Comparative Study of Religion*, 3–26. New York: Columbia University Press, 1958. (History)

Wilson, E. O. "Religion." In *On Human Nature*, 169–93. Cambridge, MA: Harvard University Press, 1978. (Biology)

APPENDIX 3

Categorizing Religious Traditions

An Assignment

What follows is the world of religion, as parsed by the editors of the *Encyclopedia of Religion*.[1] The editors divide the world into forty-three religions or religious groupings. Learn this list. Knowing this information is similar to a medical student learning all 206 bones in the human body. Such knowledge provides a structure for the religions in the world and the basis for detailed study.

The Exercise: (1) Memorize the list. (2) After learning the list by heart, write a one-hundred-word paragraph on each category that includes the following information: its geographical location (if the location is not self-evident); whether the category refers to indigenous religion(s), a world religion, or a new religious movement; prominent examples of specific religions within the category (if applicable); and characteristic beliefs of the religion or group of religions.

1. Mircea Eliade, ed., *Encyclopedia of Religion*, 16 vols. (New York: Macmillan, 1987).

African Traditional Religions
Afro-American Religions
Altaic Religions
Ancient Near Eastern
  Religions
Arctic Religions
Australian Aboriginal
  Religions
Baltic Religion
Buddhism
Caribbean Religions
Celtic Religion
Chinese Religion
Christianity
Egyptian Religion
European Traditions
Germanic Religion
Greek Religion
Hellenistic Religions
Hinduism
Indian Religions
Indo-European Religions
Inner Asian Religions
Iranian Religions/
  Zoroastrianism

Islam
Israelite Religion
Jainism
Japanese Religion
Judaism
Korean Religion
Mandaean Religion
Mesoamerican Indigenous
  Religions
Mesopotamian Religions
New Religions and Modern
  Movements
North American Indigenous
  Religions
Oceanic Religions
Prehistoric Religions
Roman Religion
Sikhism
Slavic Religion
South American Indigenous
  Religions
Southeast Asian Religions
Thracian Religion
Tibetan Religions
Uralic Religions

Twelve Guidelines for the Study of Religion

Prepare Yourself

1. Remember that religion is bigger than you are.

This statement is true (1) by definition. One of the primary definers, if not *the* primary definer, of religion is its transcendent nature (or at least its claims to transcendence). This statement is true (2) because humans are not transcendent, but fallible and limited. When we study religion, our subject matter will always, in the end, be more than we can handle. And this statement is true (3) because of the experience most of us have of our own religion. The Christian theologian Friedrich Schleiermacher describes religion as a feeling that humans have of "absolute dependence" when faced with our Almighties.[1] Phenomenologist of religion Rudolf Otto, in the introduction to his famous religious studies book *The Idea of the Holy*, says, "Direct

---

1. George Behrens, "Feeling of Absolute Dependence: What Schleiermacher Really Said and Why It Matters," *Religious Studies* 34 (1998): 471–81.

[your] mind to a moment of deeply felt religious experience. . . . Whoever cannot do this . . . is requested to read no further."[2]

2. Your subject is natural religion, not prophetic religion or pathological religion.

It is okay to think your religion is the right one, but that is not the attitude with which you should approach your religious studies tasks. It is inevitable to discover that some religion around the world is unhealthy and bad, but that discovery does not apply to all religion. As Max Müller says, "Natural religion is the greatest gift God has bestowed on humanity,"[3] and it should be studied as such. Natural religion is the raw data used by both theologians and the nonreligious to make their respective cases, but it dare not be confused with either.

3. You don't know until you observe.

One of the biggest dangers in religious studies is the temptation to project the teachings of your own religion and what you believe onto the other religions that you are studying. We are all tempted to think that because such-and-such is a part of my religion, it is a part of all religion. The findings, descriptions, understandings, and conclusions of religious study scholars must be based on what they observe in the texts and behaviors of other religions and religious people. As Clifford Geertz says, "An anthropologist's work tends, no matter what its ostensible subject, to be but an expression of his research experience."[4]

4. Practice epoche.

The term *epoche* means "to bracket" or set aside one's religious commitments in the interest of approaching other people's religious

2. Rudolf Otto, *The Idea of the Holy*, trans. John W. Harvey (1917; repr., New York: Oxford University Press, 1958), 8.

3. Max Müller, *Chips from a German Workshop,* vol. 1 (1869; repr., Chico, CA: Scholars Press, 1985), xxxii.

4. Clifford Geertz, *Islam Observed: Religious Development in Morocco and Indonesia* (Chicago: University of Chicago Press, 1968), vi.

commitments in as objective and unbiased a manner as possible. Such bracketing frees the researcher to be open to discovery about the unknowns of religious behavior. *Epoche* is temporary and does not mean one's commitments are any less firm or important. As Gerardus van der Leeuw says, "It is unquestionably quite correct to say that faith and intellectual suspense do not exclude each other."[5]

Respect Others

5. Be respectful of other people and their religion.

This is not just a matter of being "nice," although being nice is important. Respecting the religious other materially affects the results of one's studies. In one of the first (and best) methodologies in the field of religious studies, Morris Jastrow observes that "even the best equipped scholar must keep watch, lest on a subject touching personal predilections and personal convictions so closely, he find himself influenced in his investigations by his preferences or dislikes." The antidote to this danger, Jastrow advises, is "to cultivate a sympathetic attitude towards the manifestations of the religious spirit, viewed as the continuous effort of the human mind to attain religious truth."[6]

6. Let people define themselves religiously.

Do not assume you know a person's sense of religious identity simply because of external factors, such as race, ethnicity, culture, or nationality. Always give research subjects a chance to define themselves religiously. Ask them what their religion is. Ask them to describe their religious beliefs. This applies not only to religious membership but also to orthodoxy. Just because someone identifies him- or herself as a Christian does not mean that he or she embraces orthodox positions on different religious doctrines and practices. When in doubt, ask. Even when not in doubt, ask. In fact, when not in doubt, make *sure* to ask.

5. Gerardus van der Leeuw, *Religion in Essence and Manifestation*, trans. J. E. Turner (1938; repr., New York: Harper & Row, 1963), 2:683.
6. Morris Jastrow, *The Study of Religion* (London: Walter Scott, 1901), 319.

7. Don't measure one religion's theory against another religion's practice.

When comparing two different religions, avoid making the comparison uneven, especially when one of the religions is your own. Too often we can slip into the habit of seeing the best in our own religion and the worst in the religion of others. Otto quotes Adolf Harnack in regard to this point: "When one compares two religions or confessions with one another, he ought to avoid the mistake which Harnack points out, when he warns against comparing 'one's own good theory with the other's bad practice,' one's own ideal with the mere reality of the other."[7] Compare theory with theory, ideal with ideal, and practice with practice—but don't mix the categories.

8. What you see as weakness an adherent may see as strength.

Muhammad was illiterate. Confucius couldn't get or keep a job. And Gautama abandoned his wife. All these statements are true, and from your point of view these facts may seem like weaknesses. But adherents see them as strengths. As Otto says about Indian *bhakti* religion, "[In India] emphasis is laid upon precisely what from our point of view is a defect, as evidence of the superiority of East over West."[8] When confronted with something that seems odd, strange, fallacious, or unproductive, remember to ask the following questions: *What do adherents think about this? How do they evaluate it? Why?*

Be Fair to the Religion

9. Spheres of exploration: Once something achieves religious status in a culture, it will always have some influence in that culture.

The history of human religion is one of contact and contestation with other religions. When two religious traditions (and their carrying

7. Rudolf Otto, *India's Religion of Grace and Christianity Compared and Contrasted* (New York: Macmillan, 1930), 59.
8. Ibid., 81.

cultures) come in contact with each other, both are changed. Sometimes one religion may dominate the other, and sometimes a new religion is formed. But the elements of both religions live on. Van der Leeuw accounts for this by saying that each religion has two forms, a father form of will and a mother form of power: "In the history of humankind, one form never completely supplants the other; and the form of the mother lives on in religion because it is alive and in our hearts."[9]

10. Sources: Some of the most telling research findings come from outside the sphere of religion.

Religious studies is a scholarly discipline that eagerly uses the findings of other disciplines to inform its own. Philosophy, psychology, sociology, anthropology—the list is long. William James, for example, makes the point that the personal unity that comes from conversion experiences is not necessarily religious: "Religion is only one way out of many ways of reaching unity; and the process of remedying inner incompleteness and reducing inner discord is a general psychological process . . . and need not assume the religious form."[10] Religion touches all aspects of life, and this phenomenon should be embraced rather than avoided.

11. Dynamic of research: Assume a balance between similarities and differences until the evidence proves otherwise.

As we begin our study of religion, we are typically predisposed in one of two ways: to think that our own religion is completely unique or that it is simply a cultural variant of other religions. Neither is true. "Our religion" has many similarities with "other religions," but it also has many differences. As Basilius says in his *Legends of Greece*: "If there is any agreement between their doctrines and our own, it may benefit us to know them; if not, then to compare them and to learn how they differ."[11] Begin a particular comparison with the expectation of finding both.

9. Van der Leeuw, *Religion in Essence*, 1:100.
10. William James, *The Varieties of Religious Experience* (1902; repr., Mineola, NY: Dover, 2002), 175.
11. As quoted in Otto, *India's Religion of Grace and Christianity*, 65.

12. Rubrics of evaluation: While most academic fields of study deal solely with categories of true and false, the study of religion includes additional rubrics— healthy/unhealthy and sympathetic/unsympathetic.

In religious studies, the rubric of truth is about the accuracy of observation, not the truth of the beliefs being studied. Moreover, accuracy of observation is greatly aided by a generosity of spirit and respect for the other as different yet the same. A rule of thumb is to always err on the side of curiosity rather than suspicion. As Joachim Wach says, "It is true that to love truth you must hate untruth, but it is not true that in order to exalt your own faith you must hate and denigrate those of another faith tradition."[12]

12. Joachim Wach, *The Comparative Study of Religion* (New York: Columbia University Press, 1958), 9.

Index

199